Communications
in Computer and Information Science   1165

Commenced Publication in 2007
Founding and Former Series Editors:
Simone Diniz Junqueira Barbosa, Phoebe Chen, Alfredo Cuzzocrea,
Xiaoyong Du, Orhun Kara, Ting Liu, Krishna M. Sivalingam,
Dominik Ślęzak, Takashi Washio, Xiaokang Yang, and Junsong Yuan

More information about this series at http://www.springer.com/series/7899

Osman Hasan · Frédéric Mallet (Eds.)

Formal Techniques for Safety-Critical Systems

7th International Workshop, FTSCS 2019
Shenzhen, China, November 9, 2019
Revised Selected Papers

 Springer

Editors
Osman Hasan (iD)
National University of Sciences
and Technology
Islamabad, Pakistan

Frédéric Mallet (iD)
Université Cote d'Azur
Sophia Antipolis Cedex, France

ISSN 1865-0929   ISSN 1865-0937 (electronic)
Communications in Computer and Information Science
ISBN 978-3-030-46901-6   ISBN 978-3-030-46902-3 (eBook)
https://doi.org/10.1007/978-3-030-46902-3

This Springer imprint is published by the registered company Springer Nature Switzerland AG
The registered company address is: Gewerbestrasse 11, 6330 Cham, Switzerland

Preface

This volume contains the proceedings of the 7th International Workshop on Formal Techniques for Safety-Critical Systems (FTSCS 2019), held in Shenzhen, China, on November 9, 2019, as a satellite event of the ICFEM conference.

The aim of this workshop is to bring together researchers and engineers who are interested in the application of formal and semi-formal methods to improve the quality of safety-critical computer systems. FTSCS strives to promote research and development of formal methods and tools for industrial applications, and is particularly interested in industrial applications of formal methods. Specific topics include, but are not limited to:

- Case studies and experience reports on the use of formal methods for analyzing safety-critical systems, including avionics, automotive, medical, and other kinds of safety-critical and QoS-critical systems
- Methods, techniques, and tools to support automated analysis, certification, debugging, etc., of complex safety/QoS-critical systems
- Analysis methods that address the limitations of formal methods in industry (usability, scalability, etc.)
- Formal analysis support for modeling languages used in industry, such as AADL, Ptolemy, SysML, SCADE, Modelica, etc.
- Code generation from validated models

The workshop received 16 regular and 1 tool paper submissions. Based on the reviews and extensive discussions, the Program Committee selected 6 regular papers, 1 tool paper, and 1 work-in-progress paper for presentation at the workshop and inclusion in this volume. Another highlight of the workshop was an invited talk by Sofiène Tahar on "Formal Verification of Cyber-Physical Systems." We organized the discussion into three sessions. One specifically on avionic and spacecraft domain. The second one on a wider range of application domains including transportation, circuits, and medical applications. The last one included work-in-progress and tool papers.

Many colleagues and friends have contributed to FTSCS 2019. We thank Sofiène Tahar for giving an excellent invited talk and the authors who submitted their work to FTSCS 2019 and who, through their contributions, made this workshop an interesting event. We are particularly grateful that so many well-known researchers agreed to serve on the Program Committee, and that they provided timely, insightful, and detailed reviews. We also thank the editors of *Communications in Computer and Information Science* for agreeing to publish the proceedings of FTSCS 2019 as a volume in their series, and Shengchao Qin and Lijun Zhang for their help with the local arrangements.

March 2020

Osman Hasan
Frédéric Mallet

Organization

Program Committee

Musab Alturki	King Fahd University of Petroleum and Minerals, Saudi Arabia
Étienne André	Université Paris 13, LIPN, CNRS, UMR, France
Toshiaki Aoki	JAIST, Japan
Cyrille Valentin Artho	KTH Royal Institute of Technology, Sweden
Kyungmin Bae	Pohang University of Science and Technology (POSTECH), South Korea
Osman Hasan	National University of Sciences and Technology, Pakistan
Klaus Havelund	Jet Propulsion Laboratory, USA
Ralf Huuck	UNSW Sydney, LOGILICA, Australia
Alexander Knapp	Universität Augsburg, Germany
Sven Linker	The University of Liverpool, UK
Robi Malik	University of Waikato, New Zealand
Frederic Mallet	Université Cote d'Azur, France
Stefan Mitsch	Carnegie Mellon University, USA
Roberto Nardone	Mediterranean University of Reggio Calabria, Italy
Thomas Noll	RWTH Aachen University, Germany
Lee Pike	Galois, Inc., USA
Zhiping Shi	Beijing Engineering Research Center of High Reliable Embeded System, China
Sofiene Tahar	Concordia University, Canada
Carolyn Talcott	SRI International, USA
Jean-Pierre Talpin	Inria, France
Nils Timm	University of Pretoria, South Africa
Tatsuhiro Tsuchiya	Osaka University, Japan
Tom van Dijk	University of Twente, The Netherlands
Huibiao Zhu	East China Normal University, China
Peter Ölveczky	University of Oslo, Norway

Additional Reviewers

Ahmad, Waqar
Gruner, Stefan
Li, Ximeng
Qasim, Muhammad
Zhang, Qianying

Contents

Invited Paper

Formal Verification of Cyber-Physical Systems Using Theorem Proving

Adnan Rashid[1]([⊠]), Umair Siddique[2], and Sofiène Tahar[2]

[1] School of Electrical Engineering and Computer Science (SEECS),
National University of Sciences and Technology (NUST), Islamabad, Pakistan
`adnan.rashid@seecs.nust.edu.pk`

[2] Department of Electrical and Computer Engineering, Concordia University,
Montreal, Canada
{`muh_sidd,tahar`}`@ece.concordia.ca`

Abstract. Due to major breakthroughs in software and engineering technologies, embedded systems are increasingly being utilized in areas ranging from aerospace and next-generation transportation systems, to smart grid and smart cities, to health care systems, and broadly speaking to what is known as Cyber-Physical Systems (CPS). A CPS is primarily composed of several electronic, communication and controller modules and some actuators and sensors. The mix of heterogeneous underlying smart technologies poses a number of technical challenges to the design and more severely to the verification of such complex infrastructure. In fact, a CPS shall adhere to strict safety, reliability, performance and security requirements, where one needs to capture both physical and random aspects of the various CPS modules and then analyze their interrelationship across interlinked continuous and discrete dynamics. Oftentimes however, system bugs remain uncaught during the analysis and in turn cause unwanted scenarios that may have serious consequences in safety-critical applications. In this paper, we introduce some of the challenges surrounding the design and verification of contemporary CPS with the advent of smart technologies. In particular, we survey recent developments in the use of theorem proving, a formal method, for the modeling, analysis and verification of CPS, and overview some real world CPS case studies from the automotive, avionics and healthtech domains from system level to physical components.

Keywords: Cyber-Physical Systems (CPS) · Formal methods · Theorem proving · Physical systems · Hybrid systems · Performance · Dependability

1 Introduction

Cyber-Physical systems (CPS) [74] are engineered systems involving a cyber component that controls the physical components, as shown in Fig. 1. The cyber elements include embedded systems and network controllers, which are usually

© Springer Nature Switzerland AG 2020
O. Hasan and F. Mallet (Eds.): FTSCS 2019, CCIS 1165, pp. 3–18, 2020.
https://doi.org/10.1007/978-3-030-46902-3_1

modeled as discrete events. Whereas, the physical components exhibit continuous dynamics, such as the physical motion of a robot in space or the working of an analog circuit, and are commonly modeled using differential equations. CPS are capable of performing two main functionalities (a) constructing the cyber space using intelligent data management, computational and analytical capabilities; and (b) real-time data acquisition from the physical world and information feedback from the cyber space using some advanced connectivity, as depicted in Fig. 1. They can be small, such as artificial pancreas, or very large and complex, such as a smart car or smart energy grid. The development of powerful embedded system hardware, low-power sensing and widely deployed communication networks has drastically increased the dependence of system functionality on CPS. CPS are widely used in advanced automotive systems (autonomous vehicles and smart cars), avionics, medical systems and devices, optical systems, industrial process control, smart grids, traffic safety and control, robotics and telecommunication networks, etc. For example, smart (self-driving) cars are considered as a highly complex autonomous CPS composed of over one hundred processors, and an array of sensors and actuators that interact with the external environment, like the road infrastructure and internet.

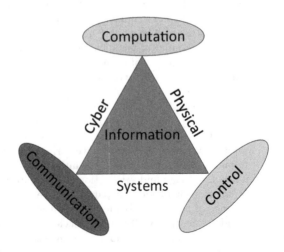

Fig. 1. Components of a CPS [2]

The main goals for an efficient design of CPS are to co-design its cyber and physical parts, and to engineer the system of systems involving the intrinsic heterogeneity. Moreover, an increase in the complexity of its various components and the utilization of advanced technologies pose a major challenge for developing a CPS. For example, in the case of smart cars, it is required to develop cost-effective methods ensuring: (a) design and analysis (verification) of its various components at different levels of abstraction, i.e., at different systems and software architecture levels; (b) analyzing and understanding the interactions of system of systems, e.g., cars' control system and its various components, such as engine, wheel, steering; (c) minimizing the cost of the car by ensuring the safety, reliability, performance and stability of the overall system. Thus, these requirements have to be fulfilled for the efficient design and analysis of a CPS.

The analysis of CPS can generally be characterised as of three types, namely, functional, performance and dependability analysis. For example, the functional analysis involves the analysis of the physical, control and signal processing components of CPS. Each of these characteristics also need to consider a hybrid behavior incorporating both continuous and discrete dynamics, e.g., the physical and cyber elements of the underlying system.

Conventionally, CPS are analyzed using paper-and-pencil methods or computer-based numerical and symbolic techniques. Moreover, most of the time is spent on designing the life-cycle of CPS and their physical (dynamical) behaviour needs to be manipulated. However, there is a lack of theoretical foundations for CPS dynamics and compositional theories for the heterogeneous systems in the tools associated with these analyses. Moreover, these analysis methods suffer from their inherent limitations, like human-error proneness, discretization and numerical errors and the usage of unverified simplification algorithms [23] and thus cannot provide absolute accuracy of the corresponding analysis. Due to the safety critical-nature of CPS, the accuracy of their design and analysis is becoming a dire need. For example, the fatal crash of Uber's self-driving car in March 2018 that killed a pedestrian in Tempe, Arizona, USA was found to be caused by some sensor's anomalies [1]. A more rigourous analysis of CPS could have avoided this incident.

Formal methods [44] have been used as a complementary technique for analyzing CPS and thus can overcome the above-mentioned inaccuracy limitations of the analysis. The two most commonly used formal methods are model checking [14] and theorem proving [35]. Model checking is based on developing a state-space based model of the underlying system and formally verifying the properties of interest, specified in temporal logic. It has been used for analyzing several aspects of a CPS [21]. However, this kind of analysis involves the discretization of the continuous dynamical models and thus compromises the accuracy of the corresponding analysis. Moreover, it also suffers from the state-space explosion problem [14]. Theorem proving [35] is a computer based mathematical method that involves developing a mathematical model of the given system in an appropriate logic and the formal verification of the properties of interest based on mathematical reasoning within the sound core of a theorem prover. The involvement of the formal model and its associated formally specified properties along with the sound nature of theorem proving ensures the accuracy and completeness of the analysis. Based on the decidability or undecidability of the underlying logic, e.g., propositional or higher-order logic, theorem proving can be automatic or interactive, respectively.

Many theorem provers, e.g., HOL4 [92], HOL Light [36], Isabelle [69], KeYmaera [73], Coq [19], PVS [68] have been used for the formal analysis (formal verification) of CPS, e,g., formal functional analysis, formal probabilistic and performance analysis, formal dependability analysis, and hybrid analysis. For instance, the KeYmaera theorem prover has been specifically designed for the formal verification of hybrid systems, thus, incorporating both the continuous and discrete dynamics of the underlying system. KeYmaera is based on deductive reasoning and computer algebraic prover technologies. It uses differential dynamic logic for the model implementation and specification of the underlying system, which is a first-order logic. Similarly, HOL Light provides an extensive support of mathematical libraries that have been used for the functional analysis, i.e., the verification of various continuous aspects of CPS, such as control systems, power electronics, electromagnetic, quantum and optical systems. HOL4 and Isabelle theorem provers provide an extensive support for the formal probabilistic and dependability analysis of systems. Likewise, Isabelle and HOL4 have been extensively used for the verification of software components, providing safety and security analysis of the underlying CPS. In this paper, we report these developments that have been done for the modeling, analysis and verification of CPS in these theorem provers.

2   Formal Functional Analysis

2.1   Verification of Physical Components

Hasan et al. [38] proposed a framework for analyzing the optical waveguides using HOL4. In particular, the authors formally analyzed the eigenvalues for the planar optical waveguides and utilized their proposed framework for analyzing a planar asymmetric waveguide. Afshar et al. [5] developed a formal support for the complex vector analysis using HOL Light and used it to formally verify the law of reflection for the planar waves. Later, the authors used the formalization of complex vectors to formalize the notions of electromagnetic optics [51], which is further used for performing the formal analysis of the resonant cavity enhanced photonic devices.

Siddique et al. [86] provided a formalization of geometrical optics using HOL Light. The authors formalized fundamental concepts about geometrical optics, i.e., ray, free space, optical system and its stability. Finally, they used their proposed formalization to perform the stability analysis of the Fabry-Perot resonator with fiber rod lens [82]. Next, the authors extended their framework by formalizing the ray optics of the cardinal points and utilized it for formally analyzing a thick lens [87] and the optical instrument used to compensate the ametropia of an eye [89]. Moroever, the authors formalized the notion of optical resonators and used it for formally verifying the 2-D microresonator lattice optical filters [88]. Finally, the authors extended their formal support for geometrical optics in HOL Light by performing the formal analysis of the gaussian [90] and periodic [91] optical systems.

As a part of the optics formal verification project [6], Mahmoud et al. [60] provided a support for the formal analysis of the quantum systems using HOL Light. In particular, the authors formalized the infinite dimension linear spaces and used it for formally verifying a quantum beam splitter. Next, the authors used their formalization of linear algebra to formalize the optical quantum circuits, i.e., the flip gate and used it to formally verify the beam splitter and the phase conjugating mirror [61]. Later, the authors also formalized the notion of coherent light, which is a light produced by the laser sources and formally verified its various properties using HOL Light [62]. Based on these findings, Beillahi et al. [15] proposed a framework for the hierarchical verification of the quantum circuit and used it for the formal analysis of a controlled-phase gate and the Shor's factoring quantum circuits. Rand et al. [75] proposed a framework implementing the QWIRE quantum circuit language in Coq, which accepts a high-level abstract model of the quantum circuits and allows the verification of their properties using Coq's features such as dependently-typed circuits and proof-carrying code. Liu et al. [54] formalized the theory of Quantum Hoare Logic (QHL) and used it for formally verifying the correctness of a nontrivial quantum algorithm using Isabelle.

2.2   Verification of Software Components

The High-Assurance Cyber Military Systems (HACMS) research program [33] was started by the Defense Advanced Research Projects Agency (DARPA) in the USA with an aim of creating a technology for constructing CPS that are resilient against cyber-attacks, i.e., CPS providing an appropriate security and safety properties. One of the major goals of this program is to create a high-assurance software for vehicles, ranging from automobiles to military vehicles, such as quad-copters and helicopters. As a part of this project, Cofer et al. [22] proposed a formal approach for constructing a secure airvehicle software to ensure security against cyber attacks using Isabelle. Moreover, the authors applied their proposed approach for formally analyzing the SMACCMcopter, which is a modified commercial quadcopter, and Boeing's Unmanned Little Bird (ULB), which is a full-sized optionally-piloted helicopter. Klein et al. [52] presented the formal verification of seL4 microkernel in HOL4, which is a third-generation microkernel of L4 provenance. The authors formally proved that the implementation of the underlying system follows the high-level specification of the kernel behaviour using Isabelle. Moreover, they also verified two vital properties of the microkernel, i.e., (1) the kernel will not perform an unsafe operation; (2) it will never crash.

2.3   Verification of Control and Signal Processing Components

Transform methods, such as Laplace, Fourier and z-transforms are widely used for solving dynamical models and performing the frequency domain analysis of systems. Generally, the dynamics of a system in frequency domain are characterized by the transfer function and frequency response, providing a relationship between its input and output and are important properties of the control and signal processing components of a CPS. In this regards, Taqdees et al. [93] formalized the Laplace transform using multivariate calculus theories of HOL Light.

Moreover, the authors used their formalization of the Laplace transform for formally verifying the transfer function of the Linear Transfer Converter (LTC) circuit. Next, the authors extended their framework and provided a support to formally reason about the linear analog circuits, such as Sallen-Key low-pass filters [94] by formalizing the system governing laws such as Kirchhoff's Current Law (KCL) and Kirchhoff's Voltage Law (KVL) using HOL Light. Later, Rashid et al. [81] proposed a new formalization of the Laplace transform based on the notion of sets and used it for analyzing the control system of the Unmanned Free-swimming Submersible (UFSS) vehicle [79] and 4-π soft error crosstalk model [76]. The Laplace transform [49,96] has also been formalized in Isabelle and Coq theorem provers. Similarly, Rashid et al. [77] formalized the Fourier transform in HOL Light and used it to formally analyze an Automobile Suspension System (ASS), an audio equalizer, a drug therapy model and a MEMs accelerometer [78].

To perform the transfer function based analysis of the discrete-time systems, Siddique et al. [84] formalized z-transform using HOL Light and used it for the formal analysis of Infinite Impulse Response (IIR) Digital Signal Processing (DSP) filter. Later, the authors extended their proposed framework by providing the formal support for the inverse z-transform and used it for formally analyzing a switched-capacitor interleaved DC-DC voltage doubler [85]. Beillahi et al. [17] proposed a formalization of signal-flow graph, which is widely used for evaluating the system performance in the form of transfer function, using HOL Light. The authors used their proposed framework for formally analyzing a die design process [16], 1-boost cell interleaved DC-DC, Pulse Width Modulation (PWM) push-pull DC-DC converters [17], Double-coupler Double-ring (DCDR) photonic processor [83], z-source impedance network and PANDA Vernier resonator [18].

Farooq et al. [32] proposed a formal framework for the kinematic analysis of a two-link planar manipulator, which describes a geometrical relationship between the robotic joints and links, and is widely used to capture the motion of the robots. Moreover, the authors performed the formal kinematic analysis of a biped walking robot using HOL Light. Next, Affeldt et al. [4] carried forward this idea and formalized the foundational support for 3D analysis of the robotic manipulators in Coq. The authors used their proposed framework for the kinematic analysis of the SCARA robot manipulator. Wu et al. [97] used HOL4 to formally reason about the forward kinematics of the 3-DOF planar robot manipulator. Similarly, Li et al. [53] provided the formal verification of the Collision-free Motion Planning Algorithm (CFMPA) of Dual-arm Robot (DAR) using HOL4. Walter et al. [95] formally verified a collision-avoidance algorithm for service robots in Isabelle. The authors mainly formalized the safety zone of the robot based on the algorithm and used it to formally verify that the robot will stop upon facing an obstacle, otherwise, it will continue its movement within the safety zone. Recently, Rashid et al. [80] provided the formal modeling and analysis of the 2-DOF robotic cell injection systems using HOL Light.

2.4 Formal Hybrid Analysis

Platzer et al. [70] developed an algorithm for the verification of the safety properties of CPS. The authors used the notion of continuous generalization of induction to compute the differential invariants, which do not require solving the differential equations capturing the dynamics of CPS. Moreover, they used their proposed algorithm for formally verifying the collision avoidance properties in car controls and aircraft roundabout maneuvers [71] using KeYmaera. Similarly, Platzer et al. [72] verified the safety, controllability, liveness, and reactivity properties of the European Train Control System (ETCS) protocol using KeYmaera. KeYmaera has also been widely used for the dynamical analysis of various CPS, such as a distributed car control system [59], freeway traffic control [67], autonomous robotic vehicles [66] and industrial airborne collision avoidance system [50]. Recently, Bohrer et al. [20] presented VeriPhy, a verified pipeline for automatically transforming verified models of CPS to verified controller executables. It proves CPS safety at runtime by verified monitors. All these analysis performed using KeYmaera are based on the differential dynamics logic, which captures both the continuous and discrete dynamics of CPS and their interaction. This logic allows the suitable automation of the verification process as well. Similarly, Foster et al. [34] proposed a framework for the verification of CPS based on Unifying Theories of Programming (UTP) and Isabelle/HOL. In particular, the authors provide the implementation of designs, reactive processes, and the hybrid relational calculus, which are important foundational theories for analyzing CPS.

3 Formal Probabilistic and Performance Analysis

Hasan et al. [45] proposed a higher-order logic framework for the probabilistic analysis of the systems using HOL4. The authors first formalized the standard uniform random variable [39]. Next, they used this random variable alongside a non-uniform random number generation method to formalize continuous uniform random variables. Finally, the authors used their proposed formalization for the probabilistic analysis of roundoff error in a digital processor [39]. Next, Hasan et al. [41] used HOL4 for the formal verification of the expectation and variance of the discrete random variable and used their expectation theory to formally reason about the Coupon Collector's problem [41]. Later, the authors extended their framework by providing the formal verification of the expectation properties of the continuous random variables, i.e., Uniform, Triangular and Exponential [37]. Next, the authors formalized the indicator random variables using HOL4 and used it for the expected time complexity analysis of various algorithms, i.e., the birthday paradox, the hat-check and the hiring problems [42]. Elleuch et al. [30] used the probability theory of HOL4 to formally reason about the detection properties of Wireless Sensor Networks (WSNs) and a WSN-based monitoring framework [31]. Moreover, the authors conducted the performance analysis of WSNs [29]. Hasan et al. also used their probability theory in HOL4 for conducting the performance analysis of Automatic-repeat-request (ARQ) protocols, i.e.,

Stop-and-Wait, Go-Back-N and Selective-Repeat protocols [40]. Finally, Hasan et al. [43] formalized the notion of conditional probability and formally verified its classical properties, i.e., Bayes' theorem and total probability law. The authors utilized their formalization for formally analyzing the binary asymmetric channel, which is widely used in communication systems. Mhamdi et al. [63] formalized the Lebesgue integral using HOL4 and used it for formally verifying the Markov and Chebyshev inequalities, and the Weak Law of Large Numbers (WLLN) theorem. Next, the authors built upon Lebesgue integral to formalize the Radon-Nikodym derivative and used it for formalizing the fundamentals of information theory, i.e., Shannon and relative entropies [64]. Later, Mhamdi et al. [65] used the probabilistic analysis support developed in HOL4 to evaluate the security properties of the confidentiality protocols. A library for the formal probabilistic analysis has also been developed in Isabelle. Holzl et al. [47] formalized measure theory with extended real numbers as measure values, in particular, the authors formalized Lebesgue integral, product measures and Fubini's theorem using Isabelle. Eberl et al. [24] developed an inductive compiler, which takes programs in a probabilistic functional language and computes density functions for the probability spaces using Isabelle. Similarly, Holzl et al. [48] proposed a formalization of Markov chains and used it to formally verify the ZeroConf and the Crowds protocols using Isabelle.

4 Formal Dependability Analysis

Hasan et al. [46] formalized some fundamental concepts about the reliability theory in HOL4 and used it for formal reliability analysis of reconfigurable memory arrays in the presence of stuck-at and coupling faults. Moreover, the authors performed the reliability analysis of the combinational circuits, such as full adders, comparators and multiplier. Later, Abbasi et al. [3] extended the reliability analysis framework by formally verifying some statistical properties, i.e., second moment and variance and other reliability concepts, i.e., survival, hazard and fractile functions. The authors utilized their proposed framework for formally analyzing the essential electronic and electrical system components.

Liu et al. [56] proposed a framework to reason about the finite-state discrete-time Markov chains using HOL4 and formally verified some of its properties such as joint and steady-state probabilities, and reversibility. The authors utilized their proposed framework to formally analyze a binary communication channel and an automatic mail quality measurement protocol [58]. Next, the authors formalized the discrete-time Markov reward models and used it to formally reason about the memory contention problem of a multi-processor system [57]. Later, the authors proposed a framework to formally reason about the properties of the Hidden Markov Models (HMMs) such as joint probabilities and formally analyzed a DNA sequence [55].

Ahmad et al. [9] developed a higher-order logic based framework for the formal dependability analysis using probability theory of HOL4. The proposed analysis provides the failure characteristics of the systems, i.e., reliability, availability, maintainability, etc. The authors formalized the Reliability Block Diagrams

(RBD) [11], which are the graphical representations providing the functional behaviour of a system modules and their interconnections. The proposed formalization of RBD has been used for formally analyzing a simple oil and gas pipeline, a generic Virtual Data Center (VDC) [13], Reliable Multi-Segment Transport (RMST) data transport, Event to Sink Reliable Transport (ESRT) protocols [12] and Logistics Service Supply Chains (LSSCs) [10]. Similarly, Ahmad et al. [7] proposed a framework for the formal fault tree analysis using HOL4. The authors formalized the fault tree gates, i.e., AND, OR, NAND, NOR, XOR and NOT and formally verified their generic expressions for probabilities failures. Moreover, their proposed framework was used to perform the fault tree analysis of a solar array, which is used as a major source of power in the Dong Fang Hong-3 (DFH-3) satellite [7] and a communication gateway software for the next generation Air Traffic Management System (ATMS) [8].

Elderhalli et al. [26] developed a higher-order logic based framework for the formal dynamic dependability analysis using HOL4. The proposed analysis provides the dynamic failure characteristics of the systems, i.e., dynamic reliability and fault trees, etc. The authors formalized the Dynamic Fault Trees (DFTs) [25] and Dynamic Reliability Block Diagrams (DRBD) [27] using HOL4. Moreover, they used their proposed formalization for formally analyzing the Drive-by-wire System (DBW), a Shuffle-exchange Network (SEN) and Cardiac Assist System (CAS) [28].

5   Theorem Proving Support for CPS

Table 1 summarizes the formal libraries that are available in various theorem provers for performing the formal analysis of CPS. For example, the formal support for the dependability analysis of systems is only available in HOL4. Similarly, the libraries to formally reason about robotics and software components are available in most of the theorem provers. KeyMaera provides a support for formally analyzing the hybrid systems. Moreover, HOL4 and Isabelle theorem provers have a quite dense library for probabilistic and performance analyses

Table 1. Libraries for formal analysis in major theorem provers

Analysis/Theorem provers	HOL4	HOL light	Isabelle/HOL	Coq	PVS	Keymaera
Transform methods	✓	✓	✓	✓		
Probabilistic analysis	✓		✓			
Performance analysis	✓		✓			
Dependability analysis	✓					
Hybrid systems						✓
Optical systems		✓				
Quantum systems		✓	✓	✓		
Robotic systems	✓	✓	✓		✓	✓
Software components	✓	✓	✓		✓	✓

of systems. Similarly, the transform methods are partially available in Isabelle, Coq and HOL4 theorem provers, i.e., only the Laplace transform is formalized in these theorem provers. However, HOL Light contains formal libraries for most of the transform methods, i.e., Laplace, Fourier and z-transforms. Also, the formal library for analyzing the optical systems is only available in HOL Light.

6   Conclusion

CPS are highly complex systems composed of actuators, sensors, and several electronic, communication and controller modules, and exhibit both the continuous and discrete dynamics. Due to the safety critical-nature of CPS, their accurate analysis is of utmost importance. This paper surveys some of the efforts that have been done regarding the formal verification of CPS using theorem proving by highlighting the aspects of CPS that have been verified using different theorem provers. In this regard, only one dedicated theorem prover, KeYmaera, has been developed for analyzing hybrid systems. However, we need to develop dedicated formal libraries in other theorem provers that can support the analysis of hybrid systems, i.e., incorporating the interlinked discrete and continuous-time features of a CPS simultaneously.

References

1. (2018). https://arstechnica.com/tech-policy/2018/05/report-software-bug-led-to-death-in-ubers-self-driving-crash/?amp=1
2. (2020). https://www.2b1stconsulting.com/cyber-physical-systems-cps/
3. Abbasi, N., Hasan, O., Tahar, S.: An approach for lifetime reliability analysis using theorem proving. J. Comput. Syst. Sci. **80**(2), 323–345 (2014)
4. Affeldt, R., Cohen, C.: Formal foundations of 3D geometry to model robot manipulators. In: Certified Programs and Proofs, pp. 30–42. ACM (2017)
5. Afshar, S.K., Aravantinos, V., Hasan, O., Tahar, S.: Formalization of complex vectors in higher-order logic. In: Watt, S.M., Davenport, J.H., Sexton, A.P., Sojka, P., Urban, J. (eds.) CICM 2014. LNCS (LNAI), vol. 8543, pp. 123–137. Springer, Cham (2014). https://doi.org/10.1007/978-3-319-08434-3_10
6. Afshar, S.K., et al.: Formal analysis of optical systems. Math. Comput. Sci. **8**(1), 39–70 (2014)
7. Ahmed, W., Hasan, O.: Towards formal fault tree analysis using theorem proving. In: Kerber, M., Carette, J., Kaliszyk, C., Rabe, F., Sorge, V. (eds.) CICM 2015. LNCS (LNAI), vol. 9150, pp. 39–54. Springer, Cham (2015). https://doi.org/10.1007/978-3-319-20615-8_3
8. Ahmed, W., Hasan, O.: Formalization of fault trees in higher-order logic: a deep embedding approach. In: Fränzle, M., Kapur, D., Zhan, N. (eds.) SETTA 2016. LNCS, vol. 9984, pp. 264–279. Springer, Cham (2016). https://doi.org/10.1007/978-3-319-47677-3_17
9. Ahmed, W., Hasan, O., Tahar, S.: Formal dependability modeling and analysis: a survey. In: Kohlhase, M., Johansson, M., Miller, B., de Moura, L., Tompa, F. (eds.) CICM 2016. LNCS (LNAI), vol. 9791, pp. 132–147. Springer, Cham (2016). https://doi.org/10.1007/978-3-319-42547-4_10

10. Ahmad, W., Hasan, O., Tahar, S., Hamdi, M.: Towards formal reliability analysis of logistics service supply chains using theorem proving. In: Implementation of Logics, pp. 111–121 (2015)
11. Ahmed, W., Hasan, O., Tahar, S., Hamdi, M.S.: Towards the formal reliability analysis of oil and gas pipelines. In: Watt, S.M., Davenport, J.H., Sexton, A.P., Sojka, P., Urban, J. (eds.) CICM 2014. LNCS (LNAI), vol. 8543, pp. 30–44. Springer, Cham (2014). https://doi.org/10.1007/978-3-319-08434-3_4
12. Ahmed, W., Hasan, O., Tahar, S.: Formal reliability analysis of wireless sensor network data transport protocols using HOL. In: Wireless and Mobile Computing, Networking and Communications, pp. 217–224. IEEE (2015)
13. Ahmed, W., Hasan, O., Tahar, S.: Formalization of reliability block diagrams in higher-order logic. J. Appl. Logic **18**, 19–41 (2016)
14. Baier, C., Katoen, J.P., Larsen, K.G.: Principles of Model Checking. MIT Press, Cambridge (2008)
15. Beillahi, S.M., Mahmoud, M.Y., Tahar, S.: Hierarchical verification of quantum circuits. In: Rayadurgam, S., Tkachuk, O. (eds.) NFM 2016. LNCS, vol. 9690, pp. 344–352. Springer, Cham (2016). https://doi.org/10.1007/978-3-319-40648-0_26
16. Beillahi, S.M., Siddique, U., Tahar, S.: Towards the Application of Formal Methods in Process Engineering. In: Fun With Formal Methods, pp. 1–11 (2014)
17. Beillahi, S.M., Siddique, U., Tahar, S.: Formal analysis of power electronic systems. In: Butler, M., Conchon, S., Zaïdi, F. (eds.) ICFEM 2015. LNCS, vol. 9407, pp. 270–286. Springer, Cham (2015). https://doi.org/10.1007/978-3-319-25423-4_17
18. Beillahi, S.M., Siddique, U., Tahar, S.: Formal analysis of engineering systems based on signal-flow-graph theory. In: Bogomolov, S., Martel, M., Prabhakar, P. (eds.) NSV 2016. LNCS, vol. 10152, pp. 31–46. Springer, Cham (2017). https://doi.org/10.1007/978-3-319-54292-8_3
19. Bertot, Y., Castéran, P.: Interactive Theorem Proving and Program Development: Coq'Art: the Calculus of Inductive Constructions. Springer, Heidelberg (2013). https://doi.org/10.1007/978-3-662-07964-5
20. Bohrer, B., Tan, Y.K., Mitsch, S., Myreen, M.O., Platzer, A.: VeriPhy: verified controller executables from verified cyber-physical system models. In: Programming Language Design and Implementation, pp. 617–630 (2018)
21. Clarke, E.M., Zuliani, P.: Statistical model checking for cyber-physical systems. In: Bultan, T., Hsiung, P.-A. (eds.) ATVA 2011. LNCS, vol. 6996, pp. 1–12. Springer, Heidelberg (2011). https://doi.org/10.1007/978-3-642-24372-1_1
22. Cofer, D., et al.: A formal approach to constructing secure air vehicle software. Computer **51**(11), 14–23 (2018)
23. Durán, A.J., Pérez, M., Varona, J.L.: Misfortunes of a mathematicians' Trio using computer algebra systems: can we trust? CoRR abs/1312.3270 (2013)
24. Eberl, M., Hölzl, J., Nipkow, T.: A verified compiler for probability density functions. In: Vitek, J. (ed.) ESOP 2015. LNCS, vol. 9032, pp. 80–104. Springer, Heidelberg (2015). https://doi.org/10.1007/978-3-662-46669-8_4
25. Elderhalli, Y., Ahmad, W., Hasan, O., Tahar, S.: Probabilistic analysis of dynamic fault trees using HOL theorem proving. J. Appl. Logic-IfCoLog J. Logics Appl. **6**(3), 469–512 (2019)
26. Elderhalli, Y., Hasan, O., Ahmad, W., Tahar, S.: Formal dynamic fault trees analysis using an integration of theorem proving and model checking. In: Dutle, A., Muñoz, C., Narkawicz, A. (eds.) NFM 2018. LNCS, vol. 10811, pp. 139–156. Springer, Cham (2018). https://doi.org/10.1007/978-3-319-77935-5_10

27. Elderhalli, Y., Hasan, O., Tahar, S.: A formally verified algebraic approach for dynamic reliability block diagrams. In: Ait-Ameur, Y., Qin, S. (eds.) ICFEM 2019. LNCS, vol. 11852, pp. 253–269. Springer, Cham (2019). https://doi.org/10.1007/978-3-030-32409-4_16

28. Elderhalli, Y., Hasan, O., Tahar, S.: A methodology for the formal verification of dynamic fault trees using HOL theorem proving. IEEE Access **7**, 136176–136192 (2019)

29. Elleuch, M., Hasan, O., Tahar, S., Abid, M.: Towards the formal performance analysis of wireless sensor networks. In: Enabling Technologies: Infrastructure for Collaborative Enterprises, pp. 365–370. IEEE (2013)

30. Elleuch, M., Hasan, O., Tahar, S., Abid, M.: Formal probabilistic analysis of detection properties in wireless sensor networks. Formal Aspects Comput. **27**(1), 79–102 (2015)

31. Elleuch, M., Hasan, O., Tahar, S., Abid, M.: Formal probabilistic analysis of a WSN-based monitoring framework for IoT Applications. In: Artho, C., Ölveczky, P.C. (eds.) FTSCS 2016. CCIS, vol. 694, pp. 93–108. Springer, Cham (2017). https://doi.org/10.1007/978-3-319-53946-1_6

32. Farooq, B., Hasan, O., Iqbal, S.: Formal kinematic analysis of the two-link planar manipulator. In: Groves, L., Sun, J. (eds.) ICFEM 2013. LNCS, vol. 8144, pp. 347–362. Springer, Heidelberg (2013). https://doi.org/10.1007/978-3-642-41202-8_23

33. Fisher, K., Launchbury, J., Richards, R.: The HACMS program: using formal methods to eliminate exploitable bugs. Philos. Trans. Roy. Soc. A Math. Phys. Eng. Sci. **375**(2104), 20150401 (2017)

34. Foster, S., Woodcock, J.: Towards verification of cyber-physical systems with UTP and Isabelle/HOL. In: Gibson-Robinson, T., Hopcroft, P., Lazić, R. (eds.) Concurrency, Security, and Puzzles. LNCS, vol. 10160, pp. 39–64. Springer, Cham (2017). https://doi.org/10.1007/978-3-319-51046-0_3

35. Harrison, J.: Handbook of Practical Logic and Automated Reasoning. Cambridge University Press, Cambridge (2009)

36. Harrison, J.: HOL light: a tutorial introduction. In: Srivas, M., Camilleri, A. (eds.) FMCAD 1996. LNCS, vol. 1166, pp. 265–269. Springer, Heidelberg (1996). https://doi.org/10.1007/BFb0031814

37. Hasan, O., Abbasi, N., Akbarpour, B., Tahar, S., Akbarpour, R.: Formal reasoning about expectation properties for continuous random variables. In: Cavalcanti, A., Dams, D.R. (eds.) FM 2009. LNCS, vol. 5850, pp. 435–450. Springer, Heidelberg (2009). https://doi.org/10.1007/978-3-642-05089-3_28

38. Hasan, O., Khan Afshar, S., Tahar, S.: Formal analysis of optical waveguides in HOL. In: Berghofer, S., Nipkow, T., Urban, C., Wenzel, M. (eds.) TPHOLs 2009. LNCS, vol. 5674, pp. 228–243. Springer, Heidelberg (2009). https://doi.org/10.1007/978-3-642-03359-9_17

39. Hasan, O., Tahar, S.: Formalization of the standard uniform random variable. Theoret. Comput. Sci. **382**(1), 71–83 (2007)

40. Hasan, O., Tahar, S.: Performance analysis of ARQ protocols using a theorem prover. In: Performance Analysis of Systems and Software, pp. 85–94. IEEE (2008)

41. Hasan, O., Tahar, S.: Using theorem proving to verify expectation and variance for discrete random variables. J. Autom. Reasoning **41**(3–4), 295–323 (2008)

42. Hasan, O., Tahar, S.: Formally analyzing expected time complexity of algorithms using theorem proving. J. Comput. Sci. Technol. **25**(6), 1305–1320 (2010)

43. Hasan, O., Tahar, S.: Reasoning about conditional probabilities in a higher-order-logic theorem prover. J. Appl. Logic **9**(1), 23–40 (2011)

44. Hasan, O., Tahar, S.: Formal Verification Methods. In: Encyclopedia of Information Science and Technology, pp. 7162–7170. IGI Global Publication (2015)
45. Hasan, O., Tahar, S.: Formalized Probability Theory and Applications Using Theorem Proving. IGI Global, Pennsylvania (2015)
46. Hasan, O., Tahar, S., Abbasi, N.: Formal reliability analysis using theorem proving. IEEE Trans. Comput. **59**(5), 579–592 (2010)
47. Hölzl, J., Heller, A.: Three chapters of measure theory in Isabelle/HOL. In: van Eekelen, M., Geuvers, H., Schmaltz, J., Wiedijk, F. (eds.) ITP 2011. LNCS, vol. 6898, pp. 135–151. Springer, Heidelberg (2011). https://doi.org/10.1007/978-3-642-22863-6_12
48. Hölzl, J., Nipkow, T.: Interactive verification of Markov Chains: two distributed protocol case studies. arXiv preprint arXiv:1212.3870 (2012)
49. Immler, F.: Laplace transform - archive of formal proofs (2018). https://www.isa-afp.org/entries/Laplace_Transform.html
50. Jeannin, J.B., et al.: Formal verification of ACAS X, an industrial airborne collision avoidance system. In: Embedded Software, pp. 127–136. IEEE (2015)
51. Khan-Afshar, S., Hasan, O., Tahar, S.: Formal analysis of electromagnetic optics. In: Novel Optical Systems Design and Optimization XVII, vol. 9193, p. 91930A. International Society for Optics and Photonics (2014)
52. Klein, G., et al.: SeL4: formal verification of an OS kernel. In: Operating Systems Principles, pp. 207–220. ACM (2009)
53. Li, L., Shi, Z., Guan, Y., Zhao, C., Zhang, J., Wei, H.: Formal verification of a collision-free algorithm of dual-arm robot in HOL4. In: Robotics and Automation, pp. 1380–1385. IEEE (2014)
54. Liu, J., et al.: Formal verification of quantum algorithms using quantum hoare logic. In: Dillig, I., Tasiran, S. (eds.) CAV 2019. LNCS, vol. 11562, pp. 187–207. Springer, Cham (2019). https://doi.org/10.1007/978-3-030-25543-5_12
55. Liu, L., Aravantinos, V., Hasan, O., Tahar, S.: On the formal analysis of HMM using theorem proving. In: Merz, S., Pang, J. (eds.) ICFEM 2014. LNCS, vol. 8829, pp. 316–331. Springer, Cham (2014). https://doi.org/10.1007/978-3-319-11737-9_21
56. Liu, L., Hasan, O., Tahar, S.: Formalization of finite-state discrete-time Markov Chains in HOL. In: Bultan, T., Hsiung, P.-A. (eds.) ATVA 2011. LNCS, vol. 6996, pp. 90–104. Springer, Heidelberg (2011). https://doi.org/10.1007/978-3-642-24372-1_8
57. Liu, L., Hasan, O., Tahar, S.: Formal analysis of memory contention in a multiprocessor system. In: Iyoda, J., de Moura, L. (eds.) SBMF 2013. LNCS, vol. 8195, pp. 195–210. Springer, Heidelberg (2013). https://doi.org/10.1007/978-3-642-41071-0_14
58. Liu, L., Hasan, O., Tahar, S.: Formal reasoning about finite-state discrete-time Markov Chains in HOL. J. Comput. Sci. Technol. **28**(2), 217–231 (2013)
59. Loos, S.M., Platzer, A., Nistor, L.: Adaptive cruise control: hybrid, distributed, and now formally verified. In: Butler, M., Schulte, W. (eds.) FM 2011. LNCS, vol. 6664, pp. 42–56. Springer, Heidelberg (2011). https://doi.org/10.1007/978-3-642-21437-0_6
60. Mahmoud, M.Y., Aravantinos, V., Tahar, S.: Formalization of infinite dimension linear spaces with application to quantum theory. In: Brat, G., Rungta, N., Venet, A. (eds.) NFM 2013. LNCS, vol. 7871, pp. 413–427. Springer, Heidelberg (2013). https://doi.org/10.1007/978-3-642-38088-4_28

61. Mahmoud, M.Y., Aravantinos, V., Tahar, S.: Formal verification of optical quantum flip gate. In: Klein, G., Gamboa, R. (eds.) ITP 2014. LNCS, vol. 8558, pp. 358–373. Springer, Cham (2014). https://doi.org/10.1007/978-3-319-08970-6_23

62. Yousri Mahmoud, M., Tahar, S.: On the quantum formalization of coherent light in HOL. In: Badger, J.M., Rozier, K.Y. (eds.) NFM 2014. LNCS, vol. 8430, pp. 128–142. Springer, Cham (2014). https://doi.org/10.1007/978-3-319-06200-6_10

63. Mhamdi, T., Hasan, O., Tahar, S.: On the formalization of the Lebesgue integration theory in HOL. In: Kaufmann, M., Paulson, L.C. (eds.) ITP 2010. LNCS, vol. 6172, pp. 387–402. Springer, Heidelberg (2010). https://doi.org/10.1007/978-3-642-14052-5_27

64. Mhamdi, T., Hasan, O., Tahar, S.: Formalization of entropy measures in HOL. In: van Eekelen, M., Geuvers, H., Schmaltz, J., Wiedijk, F. (eds.) ITP 2011. LNCS, vol. 6898, pp. 233–248. Springer, Heidelberg (2011). https://doi.org/10.1007/978-3-642-22863-6_18

65. Mhamdi, T., Hasan, O., Tahar, S.: Evaluation of anonymity and confidentiality protocols using theorem proving. Formal Meth. Syst. Des. **47**(3), 265–286 (2015)

66. Mitsch, S., Ghorbal, K., Platzer, A.: On provably safe obstacle avoidance for autonomous robotic ground vehicles. In: Robotics: Science and Systems (2013)

67. Mitsch, S., Loos, S.M., Platzer, A.: Towards formal verification of freeway traffic control. In: Cyber-Physical Systems, pp. 171–180. IEEE Computer Society (2012)

68. Owre, S., Rushby, J.M., Shankar, N.: PVS: a prototype verification system. In: Kapur, D. (ed.) CADE 1992. LNCS, vol. 607, pp. 748–752. Springer, Heidelberg (1992). https://doi.org/10.1007/3-540-55602-8_217

69. Paulson, L.C.: Isabelle: A Generic Theorem Prover, vol. 828. Springer, Heidelberg (1994). https://doi.org/10.1007/BFb0030541

70. Platzer, A., Clarke, E.M.: Computing differential invariants of hybrid systems as fixedpoints. Formal Meth. Syst. Des. **35**(1), 98–120 (2009)

71. Platzer, A., Clarke, E.M.: Formal verification of curved flight collision avoidance maneuvers: a case study. In: Cavalcanti, A., Dams, D.R. (eds.) FM 2009. LNCS, vol. 5850, pp. 547–562. Springer, Heidelberg (2009). https://doi.org/10.1007/978-3-642-05089-3_35

72. Platzer, A., Quesel, J.-D.: European train control system: a case study in formal verification. In: Breitman, K., Cavalcanti, A. (eds.) ICFEM 2009. LNCS, vol. 5885, pp. 246–265. Springer, Heidelberg (2009). https://doi.org/10.1007/978-3-642-10373-5_13

73. Platzer, A., Quesel, J.-D.: KeYmaera: a hybrid theorem prover for hybrid systems (system description). In: Armando, A., Baumgartner, P., Dowek, G. (eds.) IJCAR 2008. LNCS (LNAI), vol. 5195, pp. 171–178. Springer, Heidelberg (2008). https://doi.org/10.1007/978-3-540-71070-7_15

74. Rajkumar, R., Lee, I., Sha, L., Stankovic, J.: Cyber-physical systems: the next computing revolution. In: Design Automation Conference, pp. 731–736. IEEE (2010)

75. Rand, R., Paykin, J., Zdancewic, S.: QWIRE practice: formal verification of quantum circuits in COQ. arXiv preprint arXiv:1803.00699 (2018)

76. Rashid, A., Hasan, O.: Formalization of Lerch's theorem using HOL light. J. Appl. Logics-IFCoLog J. Logics Appl. **5**(8), 1623–1652 (2018)

77. Rashid, A., Hasan, O.: On the formalization of fourier transform in higher-order logic. In: Blanchette, J.C., Merz, S. (eds.) ITP 2016. LNCS, vol. 9807, pp. 483–490. Springer, Cham (2016). https://doi.org/10.1007/978-3-319-43144-4_31

78. Rashid, A., Hasan, O.: Formal analysis of continuous-time systems using Fourier transform. arXiv preprint arXiv:1707.09941 (2017)

79. Rashid, A., Hasan, O.: Formal analysis of linear control systems using theorem proving. In: Duan, Z., Ong, L. (eds.) ICFEM 2017. LNCS, vol. 10610, pp. 345–361. Springer, Cham (2017). https://doi.org/10.1007/978-3-319-68690-5_21

80. Rashid, A., Hasan, O.: Formal analysis of robotic cell injection systems using theorem proving. In: Chamberlain, R., Taha, W., Törngren, M. (eds.) CyPhy 2017. LNCS, vol. 11267, pp. 127–141. Springer, Cham (2019). https://doi.org/10.1007/978-3-030-17910-6_10

81. Rashid, A., Hasan, O.: Formalization of transform methods using HOL light. In: Geuvers, H., England, M., Hasan, O., Rabe, F., Teschke, O. (eds.) CICM 2017. LNCS (LNAI), vol. 10383, pp. 319–332. Springer, Cham (2017). https://doi.org/10.1007/978-3-319-62075-6_22

82. Siddique, U., Aravantinos, V., Tahar, S.: Formal stability analysis of optical resonators. In: Brat, G., Rungta, N., Venet, A. (eds.) NFM 2013. LNCS, vol. 7871, pp. 368–382. Springer, Heidelberg (2013). https://doi.org/10.1007/978-3-642-38088-4_25

83. Siddique, U., Beillahi, S.M., Tahar, S.: On the formal analysis of photonic signal processing systems. In: Núñez, M., Güdemann, M. (eds.) FMICS 2015. LNCS, vol. 9128, pp. 162–177. Springer, Cham (2015). https://doi.org/10.1007/978-3-319-19458-5_11

84. Siddique, U., Mahmoud, M.Y., Tahar, S.: On the formalization of Z-transform in HOL. In: Klein, G., Gamboa, R. (eds.) ITP 2014. LNCS, vol. 8558, pp. 483–498. Springer, Cham (2014). https://doi.org/10.1007/978-3-319-08970-6_31

85. Siddique, U., Mahmoud, M.Y., Tahar, S.: Formal analysis of discrete-time systems using Z-transform. J. Appl. Logics-IFCoLog J. Logics Appl. 5(4), 875–906 (2018)

86. Siddique, U., Tahar, S.: A framework for formal reasoning about geometrical optics. In: Watt, S.M., Davenport, J.H., Sexton, A.P., Sojka, P., Urban, J. (eds.) CICM 2014. LNCS (LNAI), vol. 8543, pp. 453–456. Springer, Cham (2014). https://doi.org/10.1007/978-3-319-08434-3_38

87. Siddique, U., Tahar, S.: Towards ray optics formalization of optical imaging systems. In: Information Reuse and Integration, pp. 378–385. IEEE (2014)

88. Siddique, U., Tahar, S.: Towards the formal analysis of microresonators based photonic systems. In: Design, Automation & Test in Europe, pp. 1–6. IEEE/ACM (2014)

89. Siddique, U., Tahar, S.: On the formalization of cardinal points of optical systems. In: Bouabana-Tebibel, T., Rubin, S.H. (eds.) Formalisms for Reuse and Systems Integration. AISC, vol. 346, pp. 79–102. Springer, Cham (2015). https://doi.org/10.1007/978-3-319-16577-6_4

90. Siddique, U., Tahar, S.: On the formal analysis of gaussian optical systems in HOL. Formal Aspects Comput. 28(5), 881–907 (2016)

91. Siddique, U., Tahar, S.: Formal verification of stability and chaos in periodic optical systems. J. Comput. Syst. Sci. 88, 271–289 (2017)

92. Slind, K., Norrish, M.: A brief overview of HOL4. In: Mohamed, O.A., Muñoz, C., Tahar, S. (eds.) TPHOLs 2008. LNCS, vol. 5170, pp. 28–32. Springer, Heidelberg (2008). https://doi.org/10.1007/978-3-540-71067-7_6

93. Taqdees, S.H., Hasan, O.: Formalization of laplace transform using the multivariable calculus theory of HOL-light. In: McMillan, K., Middeldorp, A., Voronkov, A. (eds.) LPAR 2013. LNCS, vol. 8312, pp. 744–758. Springer, Heidelberg (2013). https://doi.org/10.1007/978-3-642-45221-5_50

94. Taqdees, S.H., Hasan, O.: Formally verifying transfer functions of linear analog circuits. IEEE Des. Test 34(5), 30–37 (2017)

95. Walter, D., Täubig, H., Lüth, C.: Experiences in applying formal verification in robotics. In: Schoitsch, E. (ed.) SAFECOMP 2010. LNCS, vol. 6351, pp. 347–360. Springer, Heidelberg (2010). https://doi.org/10.1007/978-3-642-15651-9_26

96. Wang, Y., Chen, G.: Formalization of Laplace transform in COQ. In: Dependable Systems and Their Applications, pp. 13–21. IEEE (2017)

97. Wu, A., Shi, Z., Yang, X., Guan, Y., Li, Y., Song, X.: Formalization and analysis of Jacobian matrix in screw theory and its application in kinematic singularity. In: Intelligent Robots and Systems, pp. 2835–2842. IEEE (2017)

Avionics and Spacecraft

Formal Development of Multi-Purpose Interactive Application (MPIA) for ARINC 661

Neeraj Kumar Singh[1(✉)], Yamine Aït-Ameur[1], Dominique Méry[2], David Navarre[3], Philippe Palanque[3], and Marc Pantel[1]

[1] INPT-ENSEEIHT/IRIT, University of Toulouse, Toulouse, France
{neeraj.singh,yamine.aitameur,marc.pantel}@toulouse-inp.fr
[2] LORIA, Université de Lorraine and Telecom Nancy, Nancy, France
dominique.mery@loria.fr
[3] IRIT, Université de Toulouse, Toulouse, France
{navarre,palanque}@irit.fr

Abstract. This paper reports our experience for developing Human-Machine Interface (HMI) complying with ARINC 661 specification standard for interactive cockpits applications using formal methods. This development relies on the FLUID modelling language, we have proposed and formally defined in the FORMEDICIS project. FLUID contains essential features required for specifying HMI. To develop the Multi-Purpose Interactive Applications (MPIA) use case, we follow the following steps: an abstract model of MPIA is written using the FLUID language; this MPIA FLUID model is used to produce an Event-B model for checking the functional behaviour, user interactions, safety properties, and interaction related to domain properties; the Event-B model is also used to check temporal properties and possible scenario using the ProB model checker; and finally, the MPIA FLUID model is translated to Interactive Cooperative Objects (ICO) using the PetShop CASE tool to validate the dynamic behaviour, visual properties and task analysis. These steps rely on different tools to check internal consistency along with possible HMI properties. Finally, the formal development of the MPIA case study using FLUID and its embedding into other formal techniques, demonstrates reliability, scalability and feasibility of our approach defined in the FORMEDICIS project.

Keywords: Human-machine interface (HMI) · Formal method · Refinement and proofs · Event-B · PetShop · Verification · Validation · Animation

1 Introduction

Developing a human-machine interface (HMI) is a difficult and time-consuming task [22] due to complex system characteristics and user requirements, which require anticipating human behaviour, system components and operational environment. Moreover, the design principles of HMI are different from traditional software development processes, including techniques and tools [29]. Considering every aspect of the HMI development process in a single framework, from requirement analysis to implementation, is

O. Hasan and F. Mallet (Eds.): FTSCS 2019, CCIS 1165, pp. 21–39, 2020.
https://doi.org/10.1007/978-3-030-46902-3_2

a challenging task. Since a long time, formal methods play an importa role for analyzing system interaction [5,10,11], and their use has been widely adopted in the current development process of HMI. Yet, to our knowledge there is no standard approach that can be used to formally develop and design a safety-critical HMI from spec to code.

The ongoing project, ANR-FORMEDICIS [14] where our work takes place, aims to propose a suite that can be used for developing and designing safety-critical HMIs. In this project, we develop a pivot modelling language, FLUID (Formal Language of User Interface Design), for the formal specification of HMI based on state transitions systems allowing to express requirements, assumptions, expectations, nominal and non nminal properformal models in common languages can the be derived from a FLUID model for verification, validation, simulation and animation. The derived formal models use theorem provers and model checkers for analyzing the different required functional properties, nominal and non nominal properties, and scenarios. In our work, we use the Event-B [1] modelling language for producing an abstract formal model and the Pet-Shop CASE tool [27] for producing Interactive Cooperative Objects (ICO) model [23]. The produced models are analyzed with specific developed tools. Rodin [2] is used for Event-B models and PetShop for ICO models. The analyzed models provide feedback to the original FLUID model.

We propose to illustrate the FORMEDICIS approach applying it for the development of a complex case study issued from aircraft cockpit design: MPIA (Multi-Purpose Interactive Applications). First, we develop a FLUID model for MPIA and then we generate an Event-B model and an ICO model from the developed FLUID model. In this development, we begin by specifying different MPIA components, including functional behaviour, states, assumptions, expectations, interactions, properties and scenarios. The embedding of the formal FLUID development of MPIA in Event-B preserves the required behaviour in the developed model. In the generated model, we prove important properties, such as functional behaviour, user interactions, safety properties, and interaction related domain properties. We use the ProB model checker tool [21] to analyze and validate the developed models, and to check temporal properties and possible scenario for HMI. In the ICO model, we provide the dynamic behaviour of MPIA. The developed ICO specification fully describes the potential interactions that users may have with the application. It covers both input and output aspects related to users. In the ICO formalism, there are four components: a cooperative object which describes the behaviour of the object, a presentation part, activation function and rendering function to link between the cooperative object and the presentation part.

This paper is organized as follows. Section 2 presents the required background. Section 3 describes the FLUID language. Section 4 provides the selected MPIA case study. Section 5 presents a formal development of the case study in FLUID. Section 6 and Sect. 7 illustrates the formal developments of the FLUID model in Event-B and PetShop, respectively. In Sect. 8, we provide an assessment of our work and Sect. 9 presents related work. Finally, Sect. 10 concludes the paper with future work.

2 Preliminaries

2.1 The Modelling Framework: Event-B

This section describes the modelling components of the Event-B language [1]. The Event-B language contains two main components, *context* for describing the static properties of a system using *carrier sets* s, *constants* c, *axioms* $A(s, c)$ and *theorems* $T_c(s, c)$, and *machine* for describing behavioural properties of a system using *variables* v, *invariants* $I(s, c, v)$, *theorems* $T_m(s, c, v)$, *variants* $V(s, c, v)$ and *events evt*. A context can be extended by another context, a machine can be refined by another machine and a machine can use *sees* relation to include other contexts.

An Event-B model is characterized by a list of *state variables* possibly modified by a list of *events*. A set of invariants $I(s, c, v)$ shows typing invariants and the required safety properties that must be preserved by the defined system. A set of events presents a state transition in which each event is composed of guard(s) $G(s, c, v, x)$ and action(s) $v : |BA(s, c, v, x, v')$. A *guard* is a predicate, built on state variables, for enabling the event's *action(s)*. An *action* is a generalized substitution that describes the ways one or several state variables are modified by the occurrence of an event.

The Event-B modelling language supports the *correct by construction* approach to design an abstract model and a series of refined models for developing any large and complex system. Refinements, introduced by the REFINES clause, transform an abstract model to a more concrete version by modifying the state description. A refinement allows modelling a system gradually by introducing safety properties at various refinement levels. New variables and new events may be introduced in a new refinement level. These refinements preserve the relation between the refining model and its corresponding refined concrete model, while introducing new events and variables to specify more concrete behavior of a system. The defined abstract and concrete state variables are linked by introducing the *gluing invariants*. The generated proof obligations ensure that each abstract event is correctly refined by its concrete version.

Rodin [2] is an integrated development environment (IDE) for the Event-B modelling language based on Eclipse. It includes project management, stepwise model development, proof assistance, model checking, animation and automatic code generation. Once an Event-B model is modelled and syntactically checked on the Rodin platform then a set of proof obligations (POs) is generated using the Rodin proof engine. Event-B supports different kinds of proof obligations, such as invariant preservation, non-deterministic action feasibility, guard strengthening in refinements, simulation, variant, well-definedness etc. More details related to the modelling language and proof obligations can be found in [1].

2.2 ICO Notation and PetShop CASE Tool

This section recalls the main features of the Interactive Cooperative Objects (ICOs) formal description technique used for modelling software of interactive systems. ICO is dedicated to the specification of interactive systems [23]. It uses concepts borrowed from the object-oriented approach (dynamic instantiation, classification, encapsulation, inheritance, client/server relationship) to describe the structural or static aspects of systems, and uses high-level Petri nets to describe their dynamic or behavioural aspects.

ICOs are dedicated to the modelling and the implementation of event-driven interfaces, using several communicating objects to model the system, where both behavior of objects and communication protocol between objects are described by the Petri net dialect called Cooperative Objects (CO). In the ICO formalism, an object is an entity featuring four components: a cooperative object which describes the behavior of the object, a presentation part (i.e. the graphical interface), and two functions (the activation function and the rendering function) which make the link between the cooperative object and the presentation part.

An ICO specification fully describes the potential interactions that users may have with the application. The specification encompasses both the "input" aspects of the interaction (i.e. how user actions impact on the inner state of the application, and which actions are enabled at any given time) and its "output" aspects (i.e. when and how the application displays information relevant to the user). These aspects are expressed by means of the activation function (for input) and the rendering function (for output). ICOs description do not integrate graphical rendering of information and objects. This is usually delegated to Java code or to other description techniques such as UsiXML [9]. The ICO notation is fully supported by a CASE tool called PetShop [27]. All the models presented in the next sections have been edited and simulated using PetShop. Some formal analysis is also supported by the tool but limited to the underlying Petri net, removing the specificities brought by the high-level Petri net model.

3   FLUID Language

The FLUID language[1] developed in the FORMEDICIS project is organized in three main parts to describe *static, dynamic* and *requirements*. The static part defines type definition, constant, sets and the required features for interactions. The dynamic part defines a state-transition system for describing interactive system. The requirements part expresses the required behaviour, including user tasks and scenarios. A FLUID model is an INTERACTION module which is composed of six sections (see Fig. 1). The first three sections, DECLARATION, ASSUMPTIONS and EXPECTATIONS, describe the static part of a model. The following STATE and EVENT sections describe the dynamic part of a model, and the last REQUIREMENT section describes the requirement part of a model. The DECLARATION section allows to define new typing information that can be used to describe a HMI model.

The typing information may depend on generic and abstract types, such as *sets*, *constants*, *enumerated sets*, and *natural* and *integer numbers*. The STATE section declares a list of variables, which are classified as $Input$, $Output$, $SysInput$ and $SysOutput$. The interactions between system and user can be characterized by the $Input$ and $Output$ variables while the interactions between system components can be characterized by $SysInput$ and $SysOutput$ variables. Note that all these variables can be tagged using domain knowledge concepts borrowed from an external knowledge.

---

[1] Deliverable D1.1a: Language specification Preliminary version.

Model using the @tag (i.e. Enabled, Visible, Checked, Colors) to make explicit the HMI domain properties of HMI components. The EVENT section describes a set of events to present a state transition in which each event is composed of guard(s) and action(s). All these events are also categorized as *acquisition*, *presentation* and *internal* events. Acquisition events model acquisition operations of HMI component by modifying the acquisition state variables. Similarly, the presentation events model presentation operation by modifying the presentation state variables. The internal events model internal operations by modifying the internal state variables. These classification of events allow to check reactive properties, such as one stating that every acquisition is immediately followed by a presentation event or an internal event. This section also contains an INITIALISATION event to set initial values.

```
INTERACTION Component_Name
  DECLARATION
    SETS s
    CONSTANT c
  STATE
    Input State Variables
    Output State Variables
    SysInput State Variables
    SysOutput State Variables
      v            //A variable without @tag
      v@tag        //A variables with domain specific @tag
  EVENTS
    INIT
    Acquisition Events
    Presentation Events
    Internal Events
      Event evt@tag[x]
      where
        G(s, c, v, x, v@tag, x@tag)
      then
        v : |BA(s, c, v, x, v', v@tag, x@tag, v'@tag)
      end
  ASSUMPTIONS
    A(s, c)
  EXPECTATIONS
    Exp(s, c)
  REQUIREMENTS
    PROPERTIES
      Prop(s, c, v, v@tag)
    SCENARIOS
      NOMINAL
        SC(s, c, v, v@tag)
      NON NOMINAL
        NSC(s, c, v, v@tag)
END Component_Name
```

Fig. 1. FLUID model structure

The ASSUMPTIONS section introduces the required assumptions related to environment that includes the user and machine agents. These assumptions can be expressed as logical properties to express HMI properties. The EXPECTATIONS section describes *prescriptive* statements that are expected to be fulfilled by parts of the environment of an interactive system. Note that the assumptions and expectations can be expressed in the same way, but both are different. The REQUIREMENTS section is divided into two subsections, known as PROPERTIES and SCENARIOS. The PROPERTIES section describes in logic all the required properties of an interactive system that must be preserved by a defined system. The SCENARIOS section describes both nominal and non-nominal scenarios using algebraic expressions, close to CTT [28], for analyzing possible acceptable and non-acceptable interactions.

4 MPIA Case Study

ARINC 661 is a standard, designed by the Airlines Electronic Engineering Committee (AEEC), for normalizing the definition of a Cockpit Display System (CDS) [6] and it provides guidelines for developing the CDS independently from the aircraft systems. The CDS provides graphical and interactive services to use applications within the flight deck environment. It controls user-system interaction by integrating input devices, such as keyboard and mouse.

We present the Multi-Purpose Interactive Application (MPIA) that complies with ARINC 661 standard to demonstrate our formal modelling and verification approach considering several software engineering concepts related to HMI. Figure 2 depicts MPIA which is a real User Application (UA) for handling several flight parameters. This application contains a tabbed panel with three tabs, WXR for managing weather radar information, GCAS for Ground Collision Avoidance System parameters and AIR-COND for dealing with air conditioning settings. A crew member is allowed to switch to any mode (see Fig. 2) using tabs. These tabs have three different applications which can be controlled by the pilot and the co-pilot using any input devices.

The MPIA window of any tab is composed of three main parts: *information area*, *workspace area* and *menu bar*. The information area is the top bar of any tab that splits in two parts for displaying the current state of the application on the left part and the error messages, actions in progress or bad manipulation when necessary on the right part. The workspace area shows changes according to the selected interactive control panel. For example, WXR workspace displays all the modifiable parameters of the weather radar sensor, GCAS workspace shows some of the working modes of GCAS, and AIRCOND workspace displays the selected temperature inside an aircraft. The menu bar area contains three tabs for accessing the interactive control panels related to WXR, GCAS and AIRCOND.

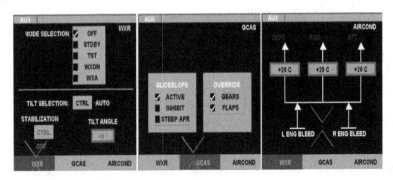

Fig. 2. Snapshots of the MPIA (from left to right: WXR, GCAS and AIRCOND)

5 Formal Development of MPIA in FLUID

We present a formal description of MPIA in FLUID. Due to space limitation, we show only the FLUID model of weather radar information (WXR). The other HMI widgets, such as GCAS and AIRCOND, of MPIA are developed in a similar way.

5.1 Declaration

For modelling the HMI of WXR in FLUID, we define a set of enumerated datatypes and a constant to represent system properties in the DECLARATION clause. Three enumeration sets are: WXR_MODE_SELC_SET for modes, WXR_TILT_STAB_MSG for messages, and WXR_ACTIONS for actions. A constant WXR_ANGL_RANG is defined a range of tilt angle.

5.2 State

In WXR model, we define several state variables in STATE clause for representing *Input, Output, SysInput* and *SysOutput* states. There are four variables to represent input or acquisition states and six variables to represent output or presentation states. All these variables associated with *tag* information (*Input, Enabled, Visible, Checked, etc.*) are defined with the given datatypes. Note that the associated *tags* are defined in a HMI metadata library, including types.

5.3 Events

To model the functional interactive behaviour of WXR,
we define a set of events,
including an INIT event in
the EVENT clause. The *INIT*
event only sets initial value
for each state variable while
the other events are used
to model possible HMI
behaviour (state changes). In
the INIT event, we show
initial state of an acquisition variable (*A_Mode
Selection*) and a presen-
tation variable (*P_check
Mode*), including *tag* details.
Other state variables and their
associated *tags* are initialized
in a similar way.

```
DECLARATION
// WXR Mode enumeration set
TYPE WXR_MODE_SELC_SET = enumeration (M_OFF, STDBY, TST, WXON, WXA)
// WXR Tilt and Stabilisation message enumeration set
TYPE WXR_TILT_STAB_MSG = enumeration (ON, OFF, AUTO, MANUAL)
// WXR Tilt angle range
CONSTANT WXR_ANGL_RANG = [ -15 .. 15 ]
// WRX actions
TYPE WXR_ACTIONS = enumeration (TILT_CTRL, STAB_CTRL)
```

```
STATE Section
// Acquisition states
A_ModeSelection@{Input, Checked} : WXR_MODE_SELC_SET // Mode state
A_TiltSelection@{Input, Enabled} : WXR_TILT_SELC_SET // Tilt state
A_Stabilization@{Input, Enabled} : WXR_STAB_SELC_SET // Stabilization state
A_TiltAngle@{Input,Enabled} : WXR_ANGL_RANG // Tile angle state
...
// Presentation states
// Radio buttons presentation states
P_checkMode@{Output, Checked} : WXR_MODE_SELC_SET → BOOL
// CTRL tilt button presentation state
P_ctrlModeTilt_Button@{Output, Enabled} : WXR_ACTIONS
// CTRL tilt label presentation state
P_ctrlModeTilt_Label@{Output, Visible} : WXR_TILT_STAB_MSG
// CTRL stablization button presentation state
P_ctrlModeStab_Button@{Output, Enabled} : WXR_ACTIONS
// CTRL stablization label presentation state
P_ctrlModeStab_Label@{Output, Visible} : WXR_TILT_STAB_MSG
// Tilt angle value in the presentation state
P_TiltAngle@{Output, Enabled} : WXR_ANGL_RANG
```

The FLUID model contains 6 acquisition events in the acquisition clause, and 7 presentation events in the presentation clause. Here, we only show two acquisition events (*modeSelection* and *tiltCtrl*) and one presentation event (*checkMode*) to demonstrate the modelling concepts related to HMI. Note that the name of acquisition event is followed by @*Acquisition*, and the name of presentation event is followed by @*Presentation*. The semantics of FLUID language guarantee that an acquisition event is always followed by the corresponding presentation event or internal event to express an interaction behaviour composed of several atomic events related to input, output etc.

The event *modeSelection* is allowed to select any mode to the input or acquisition state (*A_ModeSelection*) from the workspace area of WXR (see Fig. 2). Note that only input variable and associated *tag* value are updated through event's actions. Similarly, the event *tiltCtrl* is used to select a possible action to the input or acquisition state (*A_TiltSelection*). In this event, the actions are also used to update input variable, including *tag*. The event *checkMode* presents the state changing behaviour of a widget (radio) defined in the workspace area (see Fig. 2).

The guard of this event state that the selected widget option, acquired by the acquisition state ($A\_ModeSelection$) should not be $Checked$. The action of this event shows the selected option as $TRUE$ and the other options as $FALSE$, and the associated tag is updated as $TRUE$. Other events related to acquisition and presentation are modelled in a similar way.

5.4 Requirements

The REQUIREMENTS clause of FLUID model contains a set of required properties, and nominal and non nominal scenarios expressing expected, respectively unexpected, behaviors. In our model, we define 8 safety properties to check the correctness of HMI model. The first safety property ($Prop\_1$) states that always a single option is selected from the workspace area (see Fig. 2). The second property ($Prop\_2$) states that the acquisition event $modeSelection$ is always followed by the presentation event $checkMode$. Other properties are defined to check the interaction behaviour of HMI components. We define a nominal scenario SC_1 and a non nominal NSC_1 which are started by the INIT event that is followed by the mode selection, tilt selection, stabilization and tilt angle activities using interleaving operator ($\|$). Note that each activity is composed of acquisition and presentation events in a sequential order (;). In addition, if there are more than one possible events of acquisition, or presentation then we use optional operator [ ] to compose them. To simulate these scenarios iteratively, we use $*$ operator. Note that the nominal scenario shows possible expected HMI interactions that may occur, while the non nominal scenario shows unexpected HMI interaction that must not occur.

```
EVENTS Section
// Initialisation Event
INIT =
    A_ModeSelection := OFF
    A_ModeSelection@Checked := TRUE
    . . .
    // Only OFF mode is selected at initialisation
    P_checkMode := {i ↦ j | i ∈ WXR_MODE_SELC_SET ∧
    j = FALSE } ∪ { M_OFF ↦ TRUE } ) \ {M_OFF ↦ FALSE}
    P_checkMode@Checked := TRUE
    . . .
```

```
// ACQUISITION Events
// Any mode is allowed to select from WXR to acquisition state
Event modeSelection@Acquisition  =
        ANY
            mode
        WHERE
            mode : WXR_MODE_SELC_SET
        THEN
            A_ModeSelection := mode
            A_ModeSelection@Checked := TRUE
        END

// The tilt selection model : AUTO or MANUAL (to acquisition state).
// The CTRL push-button allows to swap between the two modes
 Event tiltCtrl@Acquisition  =
        ANY
            n_tilt
        WHERE
            n_tilt : WXR_ACTION ∧ n_stab = TILT_CTRL ∧
            n_stab@Enabled = TRUE
        THEN
            A_TiltSelection := n_tilt
            A_TiltSelection@Enabled := TRUE
        END

Event stabCtrl@Acquisition  = . . .
Event tiltAngle@Acquisition  = . . .
Event tiltAngle_Greater_15@Acquisition  = . . .
Event tiltAngle_Less_15@Acquisition  = . . .
```

```
// PRESENTATION Events
// Presentation of radio button: Only selected mode will be checked as TRUE
Event checkMode@Presentation  =
        WHEN
            A_ModeSelection@Checked = TRUE
        THEN
            P_checkMode:=( {i ↦ j | i ∈ WXR_MODE_SELC_SET
            ∧ j = FALSE }∪{ A_ModeSelection ↦ TRUE } )\
            {A_ModeSelection ↦ FALSE}
            P_checkMode@checked := TRUE
        END
Event ctrlModeTilt_Auto@Presentation  = . . .
Event ctrlModeTilt_Manual@Presentation  = . . .
Event ctrlModeStab_On@Presentation  = . . .
Event ctrlModeStab_Off@Presentation  = . . .
Event tiltAngle_True@Presentation  = . . .
Event tiltAngle_False@Presentation  = . . .
```

```
REQUIREMENTS Section
PROPERTIES
  Prop1 :∀ m1,m2· m1∈ WXR_MODE_SELC_SET ∧ m2∈ WXR_MODE_SELC_SET ∧ m1↦ TRUE ∈ prj1(prj1(P_checkMode)) ∧
        m2↦ TRUE ∈ prj1(prj1(P_checkMode)) ⇒ m1=m2
  Prop2 :G(e(modeSelection@Acquisition) ⇒ X (e(checkMode@Presentation) ))
  Prop3 :(e(tiltAngle@Acquisition) ⇒ (e(tiltAngle_True) or e(tiltAngle_False@Presentation)))
  Prop4 :(P_ctrlModeTilt_Label = (AUTO↦Output)↦TRUE ⇒ P_ctrlModeStab_Label = (OFF↦Output)↦TRUE)
  Prop5 :(P_ctrlModeTilt_Label = (MANUAL↦Output)↦TRUE ⇒ P_ctrlModeStab_Label = (ON↦Output)↦TRUE)
  Prop6 :(P_ctrlModeTilt_Label = (AUTO↦Output)↦TRUE ⇒ P_ctrlModeStab_Button = (STAB_CTRL↦Output)↦FALSE)
  Prop7 :(P_ctrlModeTilt_Label = (MANUAL↦Output)↦TRUE ⇒ P_ctrlModeStab_Button = (STAB_CTRL↦Output)↦TRUE)
  Prop8 :(P_ctrlModeTilt_Label = (MANUAL↦Output)↦TRUE ⇒ P_TiltAngle = (10↦Output)↦TRUE)
SCENARIOS
  NOMINAL
    SC_1 = INIT; ((modeSelection@Acquisition; checkMode@Presentation)
       || (tiltCtrl@Acquisition; (ctrlModeTilt_Auto@Presentation [] ctrlModeTilt_Manual@Presentation))
       || (stabCtrl@Acquisition; (ctrlModeStab_On@Presentation [] ctrlModeStab_Off@Presentation))
       || (tiltAngle@Acquisition [] tiltAngle_Greater_15@Acquisition [] Evt_tiltAngle_Less_15@Acquisition);
       (tiltAngle_True@Presentation [] Evt_tiltAngle_False@Presentation))*
  NON NOMINAL
    SC_1 = INIT; ((modeSelection@Acquisition; checkMode@Presentation)
       || (tiltCtrl@Acquisition; ctrlModeTilt_Auto@Presentation ; (stabCtrl@Acquisition[]tiltAngle@Acquisition)))*
```

In this model, the SC_1 shows possible interactions of WXR HMI while the NSC_1 shows some of the impossible WXR HMI interactions, for example, if an acquisition of tilt selection is followed by the auto mode presentation then the acquisition of stabilization or tilt angle is not possible.

6   Exploring the MPIA FLUID Model in Event-B

A FLUID model is translated into Event-B as follows: (1) An INTERACTION FLUID component is interpreted as a machine and a context in Event-B; (2) All the constants and sets defined in a FLUID model correspond to an Event-B context; (3) FLUID states are translated into a set of variables in an Event-B model, and the variable typing is also defined as typing invariants of Event-B; (4) FLUID initialisation event and the other events are transformed into an Event-B initialisation event and to a set of events; and (5) The properties of FLUID model are translated into Event-B invariants. Note that some properties are translated into temporal properties using LTL or CTL formula in ProB to check system properties and to animate our models. Finally, the produced Event-B model is checked within the Rodin environment and all the defined safety properties proved successfully.

6.1   Model

Context. In the translated model, two different contexts are defined, the first one contains domain specific information related to HMI while the other one is used to define static properties of HMI. In the domain specific context, we define possible *tag* information for different widgets, for example, we define an enumerated set HMI_TAG to state the tag properties of HMI states in *daxm*1. In addition, we also define three constants, CHECKED, VISIBLE and ENABLED, as boolean to define tag information for HMI widgets (*daxm*2). In the second context, we declare three enumerated sets, WXR_MODE_SELC_SET for modes, WXR_MODE_SELC_SET for a set of messages, and WXR_ACTIONS for a set of actions to specify the MPIA components using axioms (*axm*1-*axm*3). Enumerated sets are defined using the partition statement. We also declare a constant, WXR_ANGL_RANG, to specify a range (-15 .. $+15$) of the tilt angle in *axm*4.

```
daxm1 : partition(HMI_TAG, {Input}, {Output}, {SysInput}, {SysOutput})
daxm2 : CHECKED = BOOL ∧ VISIBLE = BOOL ∧ ENABLED = BOOL

axm1 : partition(WXR_MODE_SELC_SET, {M_OFF}, {STDBY}, {TST}, {WXON}, {WXA})
axm2 : partition(WXR_TILT_STAB_MSG, {AUTO}, {MANUAL}, {ON}, {OFF})
axm3 : partition(WXR_ACTIONS, {TILT_CTRL}, {STAB_CTRL})
axm4 : WXR_ANGL_RANG = −15 .. 15
```

Machine. An Event-B machine is also derived from the FLUID model that is translated straightforward. The generated Event-B model shows the HMI behaviour and possible interactions with MPIA widgets. In this model, we introduce 11 state variables ($inv1$ - $inv11$) to model the dynamic behaviour of the system. All these variables are similar to the FLUID model and are declared as *tuple* using cartesian product ($\times$). Note that each variable contains state information and *tag* information related to HMI. In the current model, we introduce a safety property $saf1$ (see property $Prop1$) to state that there is only one mode selected from the MODE SELECTION of WXR. Note that other properties ($Prop2$ - $Prop8$) of the FLUID model are defined later in the ProB model checker.

```
inv1 : A_ModeSelection ∈ WXR_MODE_SELC_SET × HMI_TAG × CHECKED
inv2 : A_TiltSelection ∈ WXR_ACTIONS × HMI_TAG × ENABLED
inv3 : A_Stabilization ∈ WXR_ACTIONS × HMI_TAG × ENABLED
inv4 : A_TiltAngle ∈ WXR_ANGL_RANG × HMI_TAG × ENABLED
inv5 : P_checkMode ∈ (WXR_MODE_SELC_SET → BOOL) × HMI_TAG × CHECKED
inv6 : P_ctrlModeTilt_Button ∈ WXR_ACTIONS × HMI_TAG × ENABLED
inv7 : P_ctrlModeTilt_Label ∈ WXR_TILT_STAB_MSG × HMI_TAG × VISIBLE
inv8 : P_ctrlModeStab_Button ∈ WXR_ACTIONS × HMI_TAG × ENABLED
inv9 : P_ctrlModeStab_Button ∈ WXR_ACTIONS × HMI_TAG × ENABLED
inv10 : P_ctrlModeStab_Label ∈ WXR_TILT_STAB_MSG × HMI_TAG × VISIBLE
inv11 : P_TiltAngle ∈ WXR_ANGL_RANG × HMI_TAG × ENABLED
saf1 : ∀m1, m2·m1 ∈ WXR_MODE_SELC_SET ∧ m2 ∈ WXR_MODE_SELC_SET∧
        m1 ↦ TRUE ∈ prj1(prj1(P_checkMode)) ∧ m2 ↦ TRUE ∈ prj1(prj1(P_checkMode)) ⇒ m1 = m2
```

Events. In this translated model, we introduce 14 events, including the INITIALISATION event. The INITIALISATION event is used to set the initial value for each declared state. All these state variables are assigned as tuples to show initial states of MPIA.

For example, $P\_checkMode$ is set as M_OFF mode and other modes are not selected from the option widget of MPIA (see $act6$).

```
EVENT INITIALISATION
BEGIN
  act1 : A_ModeSelection := M_OFF ↦ Input ↦ TRUE
  act2 : A_TiltSelection := TILT_CTRL ↦ Input ↦ TRUE
      . . .
  act6 : P_checkMode := (({i ↦ j|i ∈ WXR_MODE_SELC_SET ∧ j = FALSE}∪
          {M_OFF ↦ TRUE}) \ {M_OFF ↦ FALSE}) ↦ Output ↦ TRUE
  act7 : P_ctrlModeTilt_Button := TILT_CTRL ↦ Output ↦ TRUE
      . . .
END
```

The event *modeSelection@Acquisition* selects the WXR mode in acquisition mode. The guard of this event allows to choose any mode by selecting the option widget.

```
EVENT modeSelection@Acquisition
ANY mode
  WHERE
    grd1 : mode ∈ W X R_M O D E_S E L C_S E T
  THEN
    act1 : A_M ode Selection := mode ↦ Input ↦ T RU E
  END
```

The action of this event states that the acquisition state *A_ModeSelection* of WXR mode sets the selected

```
EVENT tiltCtrl@Acquisition
ANY n_tilt
  WHERE
    grd1 : n_tilt ∈ W X R_A C T I O N S × H M I_T A G × E N A B L E D ∧
           prj1(prj1(n_tilt)) = T I L T_C T R L ∧ prj2(n_tilt) = T RU E
  THEN
    act1 : A_T ilt Selection := n_tilt
  END
```

mode with *tag* information, such as this variable is in acquisition state and *checked*. The event *tiltCtrl@Acquisition* is also specified in similar style to model the acquisition behaviour of the tilt angle.

The event *checkMode@Presentation* is related to presentation to model the WXR mode. The guard of this event state that acquisition state, *A_ModeSelection*, of WXR mode is checked (TRUE) and the action of this event updates the presentation state variable, *P_checkMode*. The *P_checkMode* is set as only the selected acquisition mode and other modes are not selected from the option widget of MPIA (see *act1*). Other remaining acquisition and presentation events are modelled in a similar way. A complete formal development of the MPIA case study is available at[2].

```
EVENT checkMode@Presentation
ANY n_tilt
  WHERE
    grd1 : prj2(A_M ode Selection) = T RU E
  THEN
    act1 : P_check Mode := (({i ↦ j|i ∈ W X R_M O D E_S E L C_S E T ∧ j = F A L S E} ∪
           {prj1(prj1(A_M ode Selection))} ↦ T RU E}) \
           {prj1(prj1(A_M ode Selection))} ↦ F A L S E}) ↦ Output ↦ T RU E
  END
```

6.2 Model Validation and Analysis

This section summarises the generated proof obligations using Rodin prover. This development results in 44 proof obligations, in which 41 (93%) are proved automatically, and the remaining 3 (7%) are proved interactively by simplifying them.

The model analysis is performed using ProB [21] model checker, which can be used to explore traces of Event-B models. The ProB tool supports *automated consistency checking, constraint-based checking* and it can also detect possible deadlocks. Note that the generated Event-B model is used directly in ProB. In this work, we use the ProB tool as a model checker to prove the absence of errors (no counterexample exists) and deadlock-free. We also define LTL properties (*Prop1-Prop7*) in ProB of the FLUID model to check the correctness of the generated MPIA model. Note that the ProB uses all the described safety properties during the model checking process to report any violation of safety properties against the formalized system behaviour. To validate the developed MPIA model, we also use the ProB tool for animating the models. This validation approach refers to gaining confidence that the developed models are consistent with requirements.

---

[2] http://singh.perso.enseeiht.fr/Conference/FTSCS2019/MPIA_Models.zip.

The ProB anima-
tion helps to iden-
tify the desired
behaviour of the
HMI model in dif-
ferent scenarios.

$Prop1 : (G(e(AE\_modeSelection) => X(e(PE\_checkMode))))$
$Prop2 : (e(AE\_tiltAngle) => (e(PE\_tiltAngle\_True)ore(PE\_tiltAngle\_False)))$
$Prop3 : \{P\_ctrlModeTilt\_Label = (AUTO|->Output)|->TRUE =>$
$\qquad P\_ctrlModeStab\_Label = (OFF|->Output)|->TRUE\}$
$Prop4 : \{P\_ctrlModeTilt\_Label = (MANUAL|->Output)|->TRUE =>$
$\qquad P\_ctrlModeStab\_Label = (ON|->Output)|->TRUE\}$
$Prop5 : \{P\_ctrlModeTilt\_Label = (AUTO|->Output)|->TRUE =>$
$\qquad P\_ctrlModeStab\_Button = (STAB\_CTRL|->Output)|->FALSE\}$
$Prop6 : \{P\_ctrlModeTilt\_Label = (MANUAL|->Output)|->TRUE =>$
$\qquad P\_ctrlModeStab\_Button = (STAB\_CTRL|->Output)|->TRUE\}$
$Prop7 : \{P\_ctrlModeTilt\_Label = (MANUAL|->Output)|->TRUE =>$
$\qquad P\_TiltAngle = (10|->Output)|->TRUE\}$

7 Exploring the MPIA FLUID Model in PetShop

This section describes the embedding of the FLUID model in PetShop for verifying
MPIA interaction behaviour using Petri nets. The ICO specification of MPIA is executable. That allows us to get a quick prototype before its implementation. The MPIA
model is also produced in the ICO specification language from the FLUID model. Note
that the ICO model only consider input and output aspects extracted from the MPIA
FLUID model. These input and output aspects are defined by adding more precise
details for execution purpose by analysing and refining the MPIA FLUID model. In
the following section, we describe only the development of MPIA in PetShop.

Structuring of the Modelling. ICOs are used to provide a formal description of the
dynamic behaviour of an interactive application. An ICO specification fully describes
the potential interactions that users may have with the application. The specification
encompasses both the "input" aspects of the interaction (i.e. how user actions impact
on the inner state of the application, and which actions are enabled at any given time)
and its "output" aspects (i.e. when and how the application displays information relevant
to the user). In the ICO formalism, an object is an entity featuring four components: a
cooperative object which describes the behaviour of the object, a presentation part, and
two functions (the activation function and the rendering function) which make the link
between the cooperative object and the presentation part. As stated above we present
how ICOs are used for describing an interactive application using the WXR application
presented in the introduction part of the Sect. 4. We thus successively presents the four
ICO parts for that application.

Presentation Part. The Presentation of an object states
its external appearance. In
the case of a WIMP inter-
face, this Presentation is a
structured set of widgets
organized in a set of windows. Each widget is for
the user to interact with the
interactive system (provide
input) and/or for the system

```
Public interface WXR_PAGE extends ICOWidget {
// List of user events.
public enum WXR_PAGE_events {asked_off, asked_stdby, asked_wxa,
asked_wxon, asked_tst, asked_auto asked_stabilization,
asked_changeAngle}
// List of activation rendering methods.
void setWXRModeSelectEnabled(WXR_PAGE_events, List<ISubstitution>);
void setWXRTiltSelectionEnabled (WXR_PAGE_events, List<ISubstitution>);
// List of rendering methods.
void showModeSelection (IMarkingEvent anEvent);
void showTiltAngle (IMarkingEvent anEvent);
void showAuto (IMarkingEvent anEvent);
void showStab (IMarkingEvent anEvent);
}
```

Fig. 3. Software interface of the page WXR from the user application MPIA

to present information to the user (present output).

The way used to render information (either in the ICOs description and/or code) is hidden behind a set of rendering methods (in order to render state changes and availability of event handlers) and a set of user events, embedded in a software interface, in the same language as the one used for the COs interface description (Fig. 3).

Cooperative Objects. Using the Cooperative Object (CO) description technique, ICO adds the following features: (1) Links between user events from the presentation part and event handlers from the Cooperative Object description; (2) Links between user events availability and event-handlers availability; and (3) Links between state in the Cooperative Object changes and rendering. As stated above, a CO description is made up of a software interface and its behaviour is expressed using high-level Petri nets. The WXR page does not offer public methods (except the default ones for allowing the event mechanism), and this is why there is no software interface here.

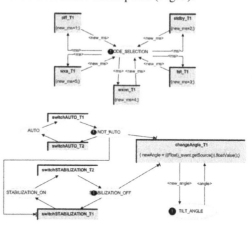

Fig. 4. High-level Petri net model describing the behaviour of the page WXR

Figure 4 shows the entire behaviour of page WXR which is made of two non connected parts: (1) The Petri net in the upper part handles events received from the 5 CheckButtons (see left-hand side of Fig. 2 for the presentation part). Even though they are CheckButtons the actual behaviour of that application makes it only possible to select one of them at a time. The current selection (an integer value from 1 to 5) is carried by the token stored in MODE_SELECTION place and corresponds to one the possible CheckButtons (OFF, STDBY, TST, WXON, WXA). The token is modified by the transitions (new_ms = 3 for instance) using variables on the incoming and outgoing arcs as formal parameters of the transitions. (2) The Petri net in the lower part handles events from the 2 PicturePushButton and the EditBoxNumeric. Interacting with these buttons will change the state of the application. In the current state, this part of the application is in the manual state and the tokens are placed in the NOT_AUTO and STABILIZATION_OFF. This configuration of tokens is required to make available of the edit box to the user (visible on the model as transition changeAngle_T1 is in a darker colour).

Activation Function. For WIMP interfaces user towards system interaction (inputs) only takes place through widgets. Each user action on a widget may trigger one of the CO event handlers. The relationship between user services and widgets is fully stated by the activation function that associates each event from the presentation part to the event handler to be triggered and to the corresponding rendering method for representing the activation or the deactivation: When a user event is triggered, the Activation function is notified (via an event mechanism) and requires the CO to fire the corresponding event handler providing the value from the user event. When the state of an event handler changes (i.e. becomes available or unavailable), the Activation function is notified (via the observer and event mechanism presented above) and calls the corresponding activation rendering method from the presentation part with values coming from the event handler.

The activation function is fully expressed through a mapping to a CO behaviour element. Figure 5 shows the activation function for page WXR. Each line in this table describes the three objects taking part in the activation process.

User Events	Event handler	Activation Rendering
asked_off	Off	setWXRModeSelectEnabled
asked_stdby	Stdby	setWXRModeSelectEnabled
asked_tst	Tst	setWXRModeSelectEnabled
asked_wxon	Wxon	setWXRModeSelectEnabled
asked_wxa	Wxa	setWXRModeSelectEnabled
asked_auto	switchAUTO	setWXRTiltSelectionEnabled
asked_stabilization	switchSTABILIZATION	setWXRTiltSelectionEnabled
asked_changeAngle	changeAngle	setWXRTiltSelectionEnabled

Fig. 5. Activation function of the page WXR

The first line, for instance, describes the relationship between the user event ask_off (produced by clicking on the CheckButton OFF), the event handler off (from the behaviour) and the activation rendering method setWXRModeSelectEnabled from the presentation part. More precisely: (i) When the event handler off becomes enabled, the activation function calls the activation rendering method setWXRModeSelectEnabled providing it with data about the enabling of the event handler. On the physical interaction side, this method call leads to the activation of the corresponding widget (i.e. presenting the checkButton OFF as available). (ii) When the button OFF of the presentation part is pressed, the presentation part raises the event called asked_off. This event is received by the activation function which requires the behaviour part to fire the event handler off (i.e. the transition off_T1 in the Petri net of Fig. 4).

Rendering Function. For WIMP interfaces system towards user interaction (outputs) present to the user the state changes that occurs in the system. The rendering function maintains the consistency between the internal state of the system and its external appearance by reflecting system states changes on the user interface. Indeed, when the state of the Cooperative Object changes (e.g. marking changes for a given place), the Rendering function is notified (via the observer and event mechanism) and calls the corresponding rendering method from the presentation part with tokens or firing values as parameters. In a similar way as for the Activation function, the Rendering function is fully expressed as a CO class.

The rendering function of the WXR application is presented in Fig. 6. In this table one line describes the three objects taking part in the rendering process. The first line for instance describes the relationship between the place MODE_SELECTION, the event linked to this place (and in which we are interested in token_enter) and the rendering method showModeSelection from the presentation part component.

The signification of this line is: When a token enters the place MODE_SELECTION, the rendering function is notified and calls the rendering method show-ModeSelection providing it with data concerning the new marking of the place that is used as parameters of the rendering method.

ObCS Node name	ObCS event	Rendering method
MODE_SELECTION	token_enter	showModeSelection
TILT_ANGLE	token_enter	showTiltAngle
AUTO	marking_reset	showAuto
AUTO	token_enter	showAuto
AUTO	token_remove	showAuto
STABILIZATION_ON	marking_reset	showStab
STABILIZATION_ON	token_enter	showStab
STABILIZATION_ON	token_remove	showStab

Fig. 6. Rendering function of the page WXR

8 Assessment

To the best of our knowledge, there is currently no full fledge development framework for covering every aspect of modelling and designing related to interactive systems. Our work project targets such a framework for interactive systems complying with ARINC 661 standard. This is the first integrated formalised framework for formal development of HMI. To support the proposed framework, we have developed a pivot modelling language, FLUID, to specify HMI requirements. Since a long time, stepwise refinement plays an important role for modelling complex systems. We also target a correct by construction design of interactive systems abstractly and then progressively develop a concrete model closed to an implementation. This progressive development allows us to introduce functional behaviour and safety properties related to system and user interactions.

The proposed language is expressive enough to cover possible functional behaviour, system input and output states, presentation, and nominal and non-nominal scenarios. The FLUID language allows us to build a complex HMI systematically, including reasoning for each step systematically considering functions, properties and domain knowledge related to HMI. To demonstrate the practicality of the proposed language, we have developed industrial examples. We have already developed the HMIs for Automatic Cruise Control (ACC), Traffic alert and Collision Avoidance System (TCAS) and MPIA. We can provide a list of safety properties, and nominal and non-nominal scenarios to check the correctness of a formalized system including interaction behaviour. The properties and scenarios derive from the usability principles, such as usability, flexibility and robustness. The presented case study covers only some of the usability principles. such as consistency, observability, tagging and task conformance. In addition, the ICO specification fully describe the potential interactions that users may have with the application to validate the dynamic behaviour, visual properties and task analysis.

Modelling an interactive system using the FLUID language provides a common understanding for the various stakeholders. In summary, the FLUID model is an abstract pivot core model of HMI for expressing interaction behaviour using state transition systems, assumptions, properties and scenarios. If there will be any error detected then the FLUID model can be modified accordingly. Many techniques, like Event-B, ProB, ICO, task analysis with CTT have been applied on FLUID model. This modelling and analysing steps can be applied iteratively to obtain a correct FLUID model. Similar to this framework, in our MPIA case study, we use on the Event-B modelling language for specifying system and defining safety properties while we use ICO for analysing possible interactions by refining the FLUID model. Note that the use of different tools provides us more confidence on the defined FLUID model. On the other hand we need to check the combination of the approach for an interactive system and the freedom of the integration of different techniques and tools.

9   Related Work

Several approaches are developed in the past years for modelling, designing, verifying and implementing interactive systems. Due to increasing complexity, formal methods is considered as a first-class citizen for modelling and designing the interaction behaviour of HMI for critical systems. There are several approaches, such as Petri net, process algebra and model checking, have been used successfully for checking the intended behaviour of HMI. Palanque et al. [25, 26] propose the development of HMI using Interactive Cooperative Objects (ICO) formalism, in which the object-oriented framework and possible functional behaviour are described with high-level Petri-nets.

Compos et al. [11] propose a framework for checking the HMI system for a given set of generic properties using model checkers. Navarre et al. [24] propose a framework for analyzing the interactive systems, particularly for the combined behaviour of user task models and system models to check whether a user task is supported by the system model. Bolton et al. [10] propose a framework to analyze human errors and system failures by integrating the task models and erroneous human behaviour.

In [5], the authors propose an incremental development of an interactive system using B methods to model the important properties of HMI, such as reachability, observability and reliability. A development lifecycle for generating source code for HMI from an abstract model is presented in [3]. The Event-B language is used for developing the multi-model interactive system supporting with CARE properties using correct by construction approach in [4]. In [19], the authors propose an approach with supported tools based on CAV architecture, hybrid model of MVC and PAC, for developing HMI from specification to implementation. In [16], the authors present a developed methodology, based on MVC architecture, for developing an HMI using a correct by construction approach for introducing functional behaviour, safety properties and HMI components.

A formal interaction mechanism is described using the synchronous data flow language Lustre [17] at ONERA. In [7], the authors present derivation of possible interactions from an informal description of the interactive system. These derived interactions are used to model a formal model of the interactive system for checking and validating the required HMI behaviour of interactive system, and for generating the test cases [8]. A modelling language, LIDL (LIDL Interaction Description Language), is proposed in [20] to describe a formal description of possible interaction of HMI. In this language, the static nature of HMI is specified using interfaces and the dynamic nature of HMI is specified as interactions. The semantics of this language is based on synchronous data flows similar to Lustre that makes the process easy for formal verification and code generation. In [15], the authors propose a formal development process for designing HMI for safety-critical systems using LIDL and S3 solver.

The project *CHI+MED* [13] proposes modelling in Modal Action Logic (MAL) and proofs in PVS for developing HMI of medical systems. In [18], the authors present a methodology to design a user interface compliant with use-related safety requirements using formal methods. In [12], the authors propose an approach for checking the required properties of executable models of interactive software in *djnn* framework. The *djnn* framework describes interactive components in hierarchical manner, including the low level details such as graphics, behaviours, computations and data manipulations.

All the above approaches are all confronted with different issues like the lack of abstraction or of formal design patterns for handling different aspects of interactive systems. Nevertheless, the main contribution of these researches and studies is to demonstrate only parts of the interactive systems such as interaction, task analysis etc. To our knowledge there is no work related to modelling, refinement, domain knowledge integration and management, scenarios, task analysis together for developing interactive systems. Our work is the first integrated framework for modelling and designing interactive systems by defining different components of interactive systems. Note that our defined language FLUID is able to model interaction behaviour, domain properties, scenarios and tasks properties for interactive systems using a correct by construction. To specify everything in one language provides a common understanding to the various stockholders.

10   Conclusion

This paper presents a formal approach for developing Human Machine Interface complying with ARINC 661. This development approach is centered around the pivot modelling language, FLUID, which is proposed in our FORMEDICIS project for specifying HMI requirements. A FLUID model consists of states, assumptions, expectations, nominal and non nominal properties, and scenarios. A formal model can be derived from a FLUID model for reasoning and analyzing an interactive behaviour of a system under the given safety properties. In our work, we have used the Event-B modelling language for producing a formal model and PetShop CASE tool for producing ICO model. We have used MPIA case study for developing a FLUID model. Further, the FLUID model is used for producing Event-B model and ICO model. The Event-B model is used to check interaction behaviour considering domain properties, including safety properties, and the ICO model is used for validating visual properties and in task analysis. Moreover, we have also used the ProB model checker tool to analyze and to validate the developed MPIA model. The formalization and the associated proofs presented in this work can be easily extended to other formal methods and model checkers that can be used for modelling interactive systems.

As future work, our objective is to define a refinement relationship for FLUID models to get closer to an implementation. Such refinement allows us to perform formal verification at the code level and we do not need to add any other verification approach. Another future work is to automate the model generation process from a FLUID model, so that a formal model can be produced and verified in any target modelling language.

Acknowledgment. This study was undertaken as part of the FORMEDICIS (FORmal MEthods for the Development and the engineering of Critical Interactive Systems) ANR-16-CE25-0007.

Funding. Funded by ANR (Agence nationale de la recherche), https://anr.fr/Projet-ANR-16-CE25-0007.

References

1. Abrial, J.R.: Modeling in Event-B: System and Software Engineering, 1st edn. Cambridge University Press, New York (2010)
2. Abrial, J.R., Butler, M., Hallerstede, S., Hoang, T.S., Mehta, F., Voisin, L.: Rodin: an open toolset for modelling and reasoning in event-b. Int. J. Softw. Tools Technol. Transf. **12**(6), 447–466 (2010)
3. Ait-Ameur, Y.: Cooperation of formal methods in an engineering based software development process. In: Grieskamp, W., Santen, T., Stoddart, B. (eds.) IFM 2000. LNCS, vol. 1945, pp. 136–155. Springer, Heidelberg (2000). https://doi.org/10.1007/3-540-40911-4_9
4. Ait-Ameur, Y., Ait-Sadoune, I., Baron, M.: Etude et comparaison de scénarios de développements formels d'interfaces multi-modales fondés sur la preuve et le raffinement. RSTI-Ingénierie des Systèmes d'Informations **13**(2), 127–155 (2008)
5. Aït-Ameur, Y., Girard, P., Jambon, F.: Using the B formal approach for incremental specification design of interactive systems. In: Engineering for Human-Computer Interaction, IFIP TC2/TC13 WG2.7/WG13.4 Seventh Working Conference on Engineering for Human-Computer Interaction, 14–18 September, Heraklion, Crete, Greece, pp. 91–109 (1998)
6. ARINC 661–2: Prepared by Airlines Electronic Engineering Committee. Cockpit Display System Interfaces to User Systems. Arinc Specification 661–2 (2005)
7. d'Ausbourg, B., Durrieu, G., Roché, P.: Deriving a formal model of an interactive system from its UIL description in order to verify and to test its behaviour. In: Bodart, F., Vanderdonckt, J. (eds.) Design, Specification and Verification of Interactive Systems 1996. EUROGRAPH, pp. 105–122. Springer, Vienna (1996). https://doi.org/10.1007/978-3-7091-7491-3_6
8. d'Ausbourg, B.: Using model checking for the automatic validation of user interfaces systems. In: Markopoulos, P., Johnson, P. (eds.) Design, Specification and Verification of Interactive Systems 1998. EUROGRAPH, pp. 242–260. Springer, Vienna (1998). https://doi.org/10.1007/978-3-7091-3693-5_16
9. Barboni, E., Martinie, C., Navarre, D., Palanque, P.A., Winckler, M.: Bridging the gap between a behavioural formal description technique and a user interface description language: enhancing ICO with a graphical user interface markup language. SCP **86**, 3–29 (2014)
10. Bolton, M.L., Siminiceanu, R.I., Bass, E.J.: A systematic approach to model checking human - automation interaction using task analytic models. IEEE Trans. Syst. Man Cybern.- Part A: Syst. Hum. **41**(5), 961–976 (2011)
11. Campos, J.C., Harrison, M.D.: Systematic analysis of control panel interfaces using formal tools. In: Graham, T.C.N., Palanque, P. (eds.) DSV-IS 2008. LNCS, vol. 5136, pp. 72–85. Springer, Heidelberg (2008). https://doi.org/10.1007/978-3-540-70569-7_6
12. Chatty, S., Magnaudet, M., Prun, D.: Verification of properties of interactive components from their executable code. In: Proceedings of the 7th ACM SIGCHI Symposium on Engineering Interactive Computing Systems, EICS 2015, pp. 276–285. ACM, New York (2015)
13. Curzon, P., Masci, P., Oladimeji, P., Rukšėnas, R., Thimbleby, H., D'Urso, E.: Human-computer interaction and the formal certification and assurance of medical devices: the CHI+MED project. In: 2nd Workshop on Verification and Assurance (Verisure2014), in Association with Computer-Aided Verification (CAV), Vienna Summer of Logic (2014)
14. FORMEDICIS Project. https://anr.fr/Projet-ANR-16-CE25-0007

15. Ge, N., Dieumegard, A., Jenn, E., d'Ausbourg, B., Aït-Ameur, Y.: Formal development process of safety-critical embedded human machine interface systems. In: 11th International Symposium on Theoretical Aspects of Software Engineering, TASE 2017, pp. 1–8 (2017)
16. Geniet, R., Singh, N.K.: Refinement based formal development of human-machine interface. In: Mazzara, M., Ober, I., Salaün, G. (eds.) STAF 2018. LNCS, vol. 11176, pp. 240–256. Springer, Cham (2018). https://doi.org/10.1007/978-3-030-04771-9_19
17. Halbwachs, N., Caspi, P., Raymond, P., Pilaud, D.: The synchronous dataflow programming language Lustre. In: Proceedings of IEEE, No. 9 in 79, pp. 1305–1320, September 1991
18. Harrison, M.D., Masci, P., Campos, J.C., Curzon, P.: Verification of user interface software: the example of use-related safety requirements and programmable medical devices. IEEE Trans. Hum.-Mach. Syst. **47**(6), 834–846 (2017)
19. Jambon, F.: From formal specifications to secure implementations. In: Kolski, C., Vanderdonckt, J. (eds.) Computer-Aided Design of User Interfaces III, pp. 51–62. Springer, Dordrecht (2002). https://doi.org/10.1007/978-94-010-0421-3_4
20. Lecrubier, V.: A formal language for designing, specifying and verifying critical embedded human machine interfaces. Theses, Institut superieur de l'aeronautique et de l'espace (ISAE), Universite de Toulouse, June 2016. https://hal.archives-ouvertes.fr/tel-01455466
21. Leuschel, M., Butler, M.: ProB: a model checker for B. In: Araki, K., Gnesi, S., Mandrioli, D. (eds.) FME 2003. LNCS, vol. 2805, pp. 855–874. Springer, Heidelberg (2003). https://doi.org/10.1007/978-3-540-45236-2_46
22. Myers, B.A.: Why are human-computer interfaces difficult to design and implement? Technical report. Carnegie Mellon University, Pittsburgh, PA, USA (1993)
23. Navarre, D., Bastide, R., Palanque, P.: A tool-supported design framework for safety critical interactive systems. Interact. Comput. **15**(3), 309–328 (2003)
24. Navarre, D., Palanque, P., Paternò, F., Santoro, C., Bastide, R.: A tool suite for integrating task and system models through scenarios. In: Johnson, C. (ed.) DSV-IS 2001. LNCS, vol. 2220, pp. 88–113. Springer, Heidelberg (2001). https://doi.org/10.1007/3-540-45522-1_6
25. Palanque, P., Bastide, R., Sengès, V.: Validating interactive system design through the verification of formal task and system models. EHCI 1995. IAICT, pp. 189–212. Springer, Boston, MA (1996). https://doi.org/10.1007/978-0-387-34907-7_11
26. Palanque, P.A., Bastide, R.: Petri net based design of user-driven interfaces using the interactive cooperative objects formalism. In: Paternó, F. (ed.) Design, Specification and Verification of Interactive Systems. FOCUS COMPUTER, pp. 383–400. Springer, Heidelberg (1994). https://doi.org/10.1007/978-3-642-87115-3_23
27. Palanque, P., Ladry, J.-F., Navarre, D., Barboni, E.: High-fidelity prototyping of interactive systems can be formal too. In: Jacko, J.A. (ed.) HCI 2009. LNCS, vol. 5610, pp. 667–676. Springer, Heidelberg (2009). https://doi.org/10.1007/978-3-642-02574-7_75
28. Paterno, F., Mancini, C., Meniconi, S.: ConcurTaskTrees: a diagrammatic notation for specifying task models. In: Howard, S., Hammond, J., Lindgaard, G. (eds.) Human-Computer Interaction INTERACT 1997. ITIFIP, pp. 362–369. Springer, Boston, MA (1997). https://doi.org/10.1007/978-0-387-35175-9_58
29. Shneiderman, B., Plaisant, C., Cohen, M., Jacobs, S., Elmqvist, N.: Designing the User Interface - Strategies for Effective Human-Computer Interaction, 6th edn. Pearson, London (2016)

Verifying Resource Adequacy
of Networked IMA Systems
at Concept Level

Rodrigo Saar de Moraes$^{(\boxtimes)}$ and Simin Nadjm-Tehrani

Department of Computer and Information Science, Linköping University,
Linköping, Sweden
{rodrigo.moraes,simin.nadjm-tehrani}@liu.se

Abstract. Complex cyber-physical systems can be difficult to analyze
for resource adequacy at the concept development stage since relevant
models are hard to create. During this period, details about the functions
to be executed or the platforms in the architecture are partially unknown.
This is especially true for Integrated Modular Avionics (IMA) Systems,
for which life-cycles span over several decades, with potential changes
to functionality in the future. To support the engineers evaluating conceptual designs there is a need for tools that model resources of interest
in an abstract manner and allow analyses of changing architectures in a
modular and scalable way. This work presents a generic timed automata-
based model of a networked IMA system abstracting complex networking and computational elements of an architecture, but representing the
communication needs of each application function using UPPAAL templates. The proposed model is flexible and can be modified/extended to
represent different types of network topologies and communication patterns. More specifically, the different components of the IMA network,
Core Processing Modules, Network End-Systems, and Switches, are represented by different templates. The templates are then instantiated to
represent a conceptual design, and fed into a model checker to verify that
a given platform instance supports the desired system functions in terms
of network bandwidth and buffer size adequacy - in particular, whether
messages can reach their final destination on time. The work identifies
the limits of the tool used for this evaluation, but the conceptual model
can be carried over to other tools for further studies.

Keywords: Timed automata · UPPAAL · IMA system · Conceptual
analysis · Network resource adequacy

1 Introduction

Modeling complex cyber-physical system (CPSs) [6] can be a challenging task,
particularly since, during the initial concept phase, architectures have to be
defined or reflected upon without specific knowledge or fine-grained models of

© Springer Nature Switzerland AG 2020
O. Hasan and F. Mallet (Eds.): FTSCS 2019, CCIS 1165, pp. 40–56, 2020.
https://doi.org/10.1007/978-3-030-46902-3_3

the functions to be executed or the software to be run on these platforms. Usually, details of the software, algorithms, and functions that are relevant to the development of conceptual platforms are not known beforehand. These elements, however, still have to be considered during the conceptualization of platform models so that enough processing and network resources are allocated to the system from the start. The challenges of modeling CPSs are even more pronounced when those are Integrated Modular Avionics (IMA) Systems [11]. Typically, aircraft implementing IMA-based systems have life-cycles that span across several decades, making it very difficult to consider or plan for future functionality extensions, making it imperative to consider for such phenomena in the initial concept of these architectures.

Given this motivation, the work described here presents a generic IMA-based network model to be used during the conceptual definition of candidate IMA platforms. The goal is to evaluate a candidate IMA architecture in terms of the applications and functions that it must support, abstracting complex network and computational system models. More specifically, the wish is to verify whether the resources of a candidate platform are sufficient to support an Avionics Application Model (AAM) that defines the resource requirements of the aircraft's platform. Also, the model permits the evaluation of alternative platform architectures, helping with the assessment of different candidate platform architectures that could potentially implement the AAM.

This work presents a model to evaluate the performance of IMA-oriented computer networks, focusing on a flexible model that can be later extended to represent different types of network architectures with different topologies and characteristics. The initial model focuses only on the network part of the resource adequacy problem. Other aspects such as processing capacity and schedulability are also important for the problem, but are not considered here.

The paper is structured as follows. Section 2 provides a theoretical background to the problem. Section 3 describes the methodology and the reasoning behind the development of the model, including the process to instantiate particular architectures. Section 4 describes the specification of high-level requirements for the system, as well as how to query the model to obtain relevant results. The results obtained by querying an experimental instance of an IMA architecture are presented in Sect. 5. Finally, the conclusion is drawn in Sect. 6.

2 Background

A recent survey performed by Wang and Niu [10] studies and discusses the characteristics of Distributed Integrated Modular Avionics Systems (DIMA) as well as the main technologies, scheduling algorithms, and methods used in the concept and design of contemporary DIMA system. In their discussion, they address the common problems and challenges encountered by engineers and designers during the development of these systems and highlight three key technologies that can help in the process: mixed critical task scheduling; real-time fault-tolerant scheduling; and real-time communication network delay analysis. The first two are concerned with how to schedule tasks to meet timeliness and dependability. The delay analysis of the real-time communication network, on the other hand, is presented as a way to ensure the real-time performance of the distributed system.

In order to ensure that all tasks, which run on different processors, can meet the time constraints imposed by the application, the communication delay between two processing nodes must be strictly bounded. The problem, however, is that computing the exact worst-case delay for such networks is most of the time impossible since realistic IMA platforms are composed of dozens of communication models and hundreds of message flows. Therefore, approaches such as network calculus (NC) [3,4] have been proposed. These approaches compute an exact, but often pessimistic upper bound for the delay of each message flow on the network. This pessimistic behavior usually leads to an over-dimensioning of the network architecture, which can quickly become expensive.

The NC technique is based on the idea of over-approximating message flows by arrival curves and under-approximating network elements by service curves. The worst-case delays are obtained by applying convolution and deconvolution operators on these curves. A recent work by Li et al. [8] uses NC to try to provide timing performance guarantees for heterogeneous multicore systems. Their work adds a virtual channel concept to each CPU core and provides a delay analysis for a typical switched network structure. The same NC approach is used by Soni et al. [9] who try to quantify the pessimism of the computed upper bounds of the NC technique when applied to an Avionics Full-Duplex Switched Ethernet (AFDX) network. In their report, the authors compare the delays calculated using network calculus with exact worst-case delays calculated using model checking. Their results show that the NC approach can introduce up to 12% percent overhead on the delay estimation due to its pessimistic tendencies.

Recent work by Xu and Yang [12] couples the concepts of Grouping Strategy and network calculus to take into account the serialization of the messages being transmitted through the same physical link in AFDX networks. They analyze the existing pessimism in network calculus and then propose a rate-constrained grouping strategy to improve the analysis of system performance. Addressing the phenomena of burst enlargement, they present a new strategy to cope with the pessimistic behavior of network calculus. Their approach, however, tends to obtain optimistic estimates for the end-to-end delay that can induce some risks to the utilization of this method in some corner cases.

Robati et al. [1], on the other hand, move away from NC and extend the Architecture Analysis and Design Language (AADL) modeling language to model Time-Triggered Ethernet (TTEthernet) based distributed systems. Their approach proceeds to define model transformations to enable the verification of the AADL models using Discrete Event System Specification (DEVS) based simulations. They present successful results for the verification of small IMA systems, but highlight that the automation of the refinement step of the model transformation is challenging and still requires some significant manual input from the user.

Finally, Zhang et al. [13] present a model for verification of the real-time constraints of IMA systems. They propose a finite-state machine mechanism to represent the behavior model of the application and the platform. The proposed model is based on specific requirements from the ARINC653 and ARINC664 (AFDX) standards. Their approach aims to address the claim that, while significant work has been made in terms of communication delay, RTOS service performance, and scheduling algorithms, these factors do not affect the system independently and the sum of their effects need to be taken into consideration in early development phases. Their approach, however, is tested with a small autopilot use case and is very likely to have scalability problems as the system grows to represent the whole aircraft.

In this work we explore the conceptual modelling of communication requirements and their verification using model checking with timed automata.

3   Methodology

The current model is structured in the form of a Network of Timed Automata (NTA) which can be instantiated according to the characteristics of the architecture and applications the user wants to investigate. This approach lets the behavior of each different component of the network model to be represented as a Timed Automaton (TA) [2] which communicates with other TAs via broadcast channels and shared variables to generate Networks of Timed Automata that can be fed into a Model Checker (MC) for simulation and analysis.

The usage of NTAs allows for a flexible and modular system that can be easily modified to accommodate new components and behaviors or be extended through the modification of the existing TAs or the addition of some new ones. This approach limits the modifications to the TA that implements the component to be changed or extended, not requiring the whole system or the interactions between the other components to be modified. NTAs also allow for flexibility in terms of the instantiation of different candidate architectures, since the TAs behaviors are independent of each other, only exchanging information through the communication channels or shared variables, different architectures can be easily implemented by instantiating different TAs, with different behaviors, for the different components of the system as long as the interface between the components is maintained. One can, for example, instantiate an TA representing a given network scheduling algorithm, i.e. round-robin, to analyse a candidate architecture and, when desired, de-instantiate this TA and switch it for another TA representing another, i.e. priority-based, scheduling algorithm, without having to re-model the whole system and the interaction between the components.

The current work uses the UPPAAL toolbox [7] as a resource for the design, simulation, and verification of the NTA model. The tool provides support for the representation of real-time systems as networks of timed automata, extending the automata representation with integer variables and structured data types, and providing channel synchronization mechanisms to support the communication between the automata.

The instantiation of an NTA model requires two different types of descriptive documents: a Global Declaration File, in which the specifics of the system, in this case of the avionic applications and of the IMA architecture, are described and declared; and a Component Instantiation File that lists which components of a library or set of TA templates will be instantiated and how these templates relate to the information provided on the System Declaration Document. With the information provided by these two documents, the toolbox is able to compile an NTA instance of the IMA architecture that was described. This model is then fed into a Model Checker which will verify if the model satisfies certain desired properties, or, in this case, whether the instantiated architecture meets the resource adequacy and timeliness requirements defined for the IMA system. Finally, the SMC provides the user with results of the verification, providing both the final status of the verification for each of the requested requirements, as well as a trace that represents the state of the system upon non-compliance. More details on each of these documents and the TA templates will be given in the subsequent subsections of the document.

3.1 Overall Network Architecture

Figure 1 illustrates an IMA network system as modeled in this work. The diagram represents a system composed of m processes, labeled T_1 to T_m, allocated to n Core Processing Modules (CPM), labeled CPM_1 to CPM_n. The CPMs, in turn, are associated to n Network End-Systems (ES), labeled ES_1 to ES_n, that are connected to each other through a network, represented by the dotted box on the lower part of the diagram. The arrows in Fig. 1 represent the flow of information, or in this case exchange of messages, between the components.

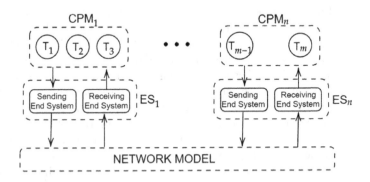

Fig. 1. Diagram of a generic network

Each Network End-System is composed of two different components, a Sending End-System, responsible for forwarding the messages it receives from processes onwards into the network, and a Receiving End-System, responsible for delivering the messages it receives from the network to the processes. It is important to highlight that each of these two components is associated, in the NTA model, to a different TA template. On the other hand, the ES itself, which encompassess both components, is not mapped to a TA, being merely a conceptual entity in our model.

Similarly, each process is mapped to a TA model that represents its behavior. CPMs are also just conceptual entities within the model and are not mapped to TAs. This representation choice is due to the fact that modeling the behavior of the CPMs themselves is not really relevant to the analysis of the network adequacy in this work since for the current analysis only the rate in which processes generate messages matter.

Finally, the Network Model represents the network architecture used to connect different CPMs. This component is, again, merely a conceptual entity composed of multiple and different TA instances depending on the type of network or architecture being analyzed.

Figure 2 illustrates how a switched network, where n CPMs are connected through an n-port-switch, can be instantiated. In this example, the switch is represented by two types of TA templates: Sending Interface TAs, which are responsible for forwarding messages to the receiving end-systems; and Switch Core TAs, responsible for the routing and switching of the messages received from the sending end-systems, assigning each message to the corresponding Sending Interface.

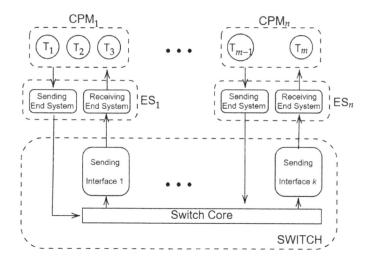

Fig. 2. General diagram of a switched network

In this model, following the interfaces provided by UPPAAL, the communication between the different Timed Automata representing the components of the network is made using shared variables. These shared variables model buffers and represent the internal storage structures that exist in most of the real physical components. This approach allows each automaton that represents a network model to forward messages to the next node in the network by writing the message directly on the other node's input buffer, modeling the delivery of a message in the receiving node. More on this behavior is discussed when the automata for the components of the system are presented in Sect. 3.3.

3.2   System Global Declarations

The System Global Declaration serves the purpose of describing the resource-related part of the IMA platform and AAM being analyzed. Here, the specific aspects of the system, such as the characterization of the end-to-end communication, the number, and the timing characteristics of the processes and of the underlying network are set. Moreover, it is also where the declaration and initialization of the communication channels, shared variables, system constants, and common functions take place.

Listing 1.1 shows an excerpt of our configuration file, showing the specific part of the file where the general variables used to describe a specific IMA architecture are located, as well as a description of their meaning. The characteristics described by these variable are specific to each architecture, detailing specific aspects of said architecture such as the number of processes, end-systems, and messages, as well as platform aspects such as the size of the network buffers and the bandwidth of the network.

```
const int N_ES =2;             // The number of end systems.
const int N_PROC = 6;          // The number of processes.
const int N_MESS = 11;         // The number of different
types of messages in the system.
const int SIZE_M = 16000;      // The maximum size of the
messages in bytes.
const int BUFFER_SIZE = 16;    // The maximum size of
network buffers in kbytes.
const int NETWORK_BD = 100;    // network bandwidth in mbps/s
```

Listing 1.1. General System Description Variables

Listing 1.2 exemplifies the declaration of a simple process. A process is described by a *Process* data structure that carries information about the worst case execution time of the process, the period in which it should be run, the end-system it is associated with, and the number and list of messages the process is supposed to read and write from the network. Each *Process* structure also caries a specific process ID, which will be fed to a generic process TA template during instantiation and allows the template instantiated for each process to access the shared data about the process they relate to.

In this case, we can see the instantiation of a process $P1$, characterized by id number $TID\_t = 1$, associated with end-system $ESID\_t = 0$, that takes maximum 7 ms to run and runs each 16 ms. We also see that process P1 makes 3 writes to network, being writes of message types 1, 2 and 3, and performs the reads of two message types, 4 and 5, from the network.

```
//A data structure representing a process and its
  charachteristics
typedef struct
{   TID_t id;                //process id
    time_t wcet;           //process WCET
    time_t period;          //period of the process
    ESID_t associatedES;        //an identifier of the
    End-System the process is associated with
    NetworkWrites netWrites;    //a NetworkWrites object that
    lists the messages this process sends
    NetworkReads netReads;      //a NetworkReads object that
    lists the messages this process receives
}Process;

//Definition of a Process P1
const Process P1 =  {1,7000,16000,0,
{3,{1,2,3}},  {2,{4,5,NO_MESSAGE,NO_MESSAGE}}};
```

Listing 1.2. Process Data structure and Definition of a Process

We now go on to exemplify how the messages exchanged between processes are defined in the context of the model. Listing 1.3 demonstrates how messages are defined in terms of a message type id, information about the sender and receiver processes, and the size of the message. Towards the end of the listing, there is an example of how a 3608 bytes long message with type id $MID\_t = 1$, that goes from process 3 to process 2, can be instantiated.

```
//A message element structure
typedef struct {
    TID_t sender;          //the id of the sender process
    TID_t  receiver;       //the id of the receiver process
    MID_t id;              //the id of the message type
    int [0,SIZE_M] size; //the size of the message in bytes
}Message;

//Definition of a message M1
const Message M1 = {3,2,1,3608};
```

Listing 1.3. Message Data structure and Definition of a Message

3.3   Timed Automata Templates

Timed Automata Templates in UPPAAL. Each automaton template that composes the final system is instantiated from a parameterized template. The parameters for each template are replaced by arguments at the moment template instantiations are declared. After instantiating the components, these have to be composed into a system, which is made through a system definition.

Conceptual Components as Timed Automata Templates. In order to instantiate and define a system similar to the ones depicted in Figs. 1 and 2 a series of templates modeling the behavior of the components of the systems have been created. The remainder of this subsection is devoted to the presentation of these templates. The syntax of the diagrams used on the representation of the templates follows that of UPPAAL.

– **Process Model:** The Process Model is an abstraction of the application processes' communication needs in this work, acting as both a sink and a source of messages depending on the location [1] the automaton finds itself in. It has 3 different locations: the *Idle* location, representing the situation in which the process is not realizing network-related activities, neither receiving nor sending messages, being idle from the perspective of the network interface; the *RetrievingMessages* location, that is reached immediately after the process leaves *Idle*, is where the automaton verifies which messages were delivered to that process since the last time it ran; and the *Sending* location, which models the state where the process has received all the messages it needed to run and done its computations, after which it creates and sends its own messages to the network before going back to *Idle*. In case a process verifies it did not receive the messages it was expecting in the *ValidatingInput* location, the process automaton communicates this error to the rest of the system through a special error communication channel and goes back to *Idle*, not going forward into the *Sending* location. Figure 3 depicts what this template looks like.

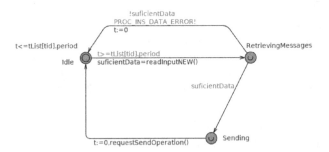

Fig. 3. The process model template

– **Sending End-System Model:** The Sending End-System Automaton is responsible for forwarding the messages generated by one or more processes into the network part of the system. The automaton is composed by an *Idle* location, in which it waits until a request is received from a process; a *Buffering* location, in which the end-system fetches and buffers the messages from the processes upon a request being received; and a *Sending* location, in which

---

[1] UPPAAL term for the state in Automata.

the automaton stays while it is sending messages to other nodes in the network. In case the end system has several messages waiting to be sent, it will bundle the messages together as to use the whole bandwidth available on the network by looping through the *Buffering* and *Sending* locations while is has messages to send. The current implementation of the Sending End-System models a FIFO message scheduling algorithm to arbitrate between the messages of several processes. Given the structure of this template, other scheduling approaches can be implemented if needed by changing the way messages are buffered and sent inside the states of the automaton, which are code that runs on the background and are not reflected on the structure of the model. This approach allows for the extension of the template to support multiple scheduling policies without significant modifications to the structure of the automaton. Figure 4 depicts the Sending End System Automaton.

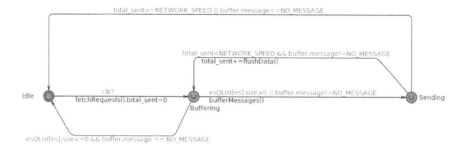

Fig. 4. The sending end system template

- **Receiving End-System Model:** The Receiving End-System is perhaps the simplest automaton in the model. Its main role is to deliver the messages that have been written to its internal buffer to the processes. This part is performed by periodically looping through the *Idle* and *Delivering* locations that compose this process. A graphical representation of the Receiving End-System is shown in Fig. 5.

Fig. 5. The receiving end system template

- **Switch Sending Interfaces:** The Switch Sending Interfaces model is very similar in behavior to the Sending End-System model, the difference being that the first interface fetches messages from its internal buffer, which is fed by the Router Core, whereas the latter fetches its messages from the processes. Due to the similarity of this automaton with the Sending End-System automaton, a graphical representation of this automaton will be omitted.

– **Switch Core:** This automaton models the behavior of a network switch forwarding engine, forwarding the messages received in its Input Buffer from the Sending End-Systems to the correct Sending Interface associated with the Receiving End-System each message is destined to. This automaton works by periodically leaving the *Idle* location to the *Fetching* location, where it fetches the next message in its input buffer. Having fetched the message the automaton proceeds to the *Routing* location, in which it finds out which Sending Interface to deliver the message to. A cycle of the automaton execution ends on the *Delivering* location, delivering the message to the correct Sending Interface, and returning to the *Idle* location by one of two edges, depending on whether the Sending Interface buffer is full and the MESS_DROP_ERROR error message has to be signaled or not. This behavior can be seen in the automaton representation of Fig. 6.

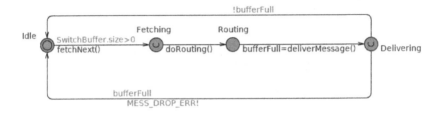

Fig. 6. The switch core template

4   Requirement Specification

We begin by describing the requirements of interest in our case study.

4.1   Requirement Definition

To evaluate a candidate platform within a conceptual architecture, we need to ascertain whether any avionics-related application(process) can ever be starved by the network, meaning that it will not receive the data it needs to run, and also whether any message will be lost due to lack of resources or inadequate sizing of the network. That leads to the specification of two main high-level requirements for the system in terms of resource adequacy and network performance:

1. **No process should ever reach a state in which it needs a data and has not yet received the data it needs** - meaning that whenever a given process needs data from a message this data should be available. The failure to meet this requirement means that, for some reason, that specific IMA platform configuration is not able to respect the communication deadlines imposed by the AAM.

2. **No network node should ever reach a state in which messages are dropped** - this requirement means, in other words, that there should not exist a network node, be it a switch, or an end-system, that continuously receives more data than it can forward or deliver where upon it completely fills its internal buffer. A node for which the buffer is full is very likely to get overloaded in an operational mode.

It is important to note that, while a failure to meet requirement 2 will probably lead to a failure of requirement 1 as well, the opposite is not true. If a given message is dropped somewhere on the network, failing to meet requirement 2, it will never arrive at its final destination, causing a failure to meet requirement 1. This is, however, just a resource adequacy problem. A message not arriving in time at its final destination, on the other hand, can be caused for multiple factors, being a much broader problem related not only to resource adequacy but also to characteristics such as the number of messages being exchanged, the number of switches between two end-systems, and the topology of the network. These requirements are, thus, complementary in some sense, allowing whoever is using the model to get a better insight on where a problem with some platform/architecture might be coming from.

4.2 Verifying Requirements in UPPAAL

In UPPAAL, models can be verified by creating auxiliary observer templates that monitor whenever a requirement is violated (i.e a bad state is reached.) Hence, two observers were created to inspect the status of the platform model during the requirement verification process. Basically, these observers are simple timed automata that listen to the communication channels for error signals sent by processes or network nodes, and change their state, to an error state. Figure 7 shows what an observer listening for processes that signaled a non-compliance to the first requirement looks like. The second observer, which listens to the network nodes waiting for signals that indicate that a full-buffer-state has been reached, was omitted because it looks very similar to the first observer.

Fig. 7. Process observer automata

4.3 Expressing Requirements in UPPAAL

The UPPAAL model-checker tool [7] uses a simplified version of a Timed Computational Tree Logic (TCTL) [5] to express requirements over the timed automata models. Like in traditional TCTL, the UPPAAL requirements language supports both path formulae and state formulae. State formulae reason about individual

states, whereas path formulae reason over paths or traces in the search space of
the model. Since the goal of the IMA network model is to verify whether a given
platform is able to serve as a basis for a given AAM with adequate resources,
we have a special interest on expressing the requirements of the network model
in terms of path formulae in terms of (non) reachability of undesired states
(expressed in formal terms as the safety of the model). In short we aim to verify
that no undesired or error state can ever be reached.

In the UPPAAL requirements language, given the TCTL logic and a formula
φ, the path formula $A\Box\varphi$ express that φ should be true in all reachable states
of the model. This type of requirement, usually expresses the so called *safety
properties*, that in UPPAAL are formulated positively, e.g., something desirable
is **invariantly true**. The two defined requirements are, then, written as:

A $\Box$ not ProcessObserver.INS_DATA_ERROR
A $\Box$ not NodeObserver.MESS_DROP_ERROR

5   Model Assessment

This section presents the analysis of an abstract networking platform architecture and an application characterised by a mapping to the platform. We then
formally verify the requirements mentioned in Sect. 4 and discuss the findings of
the formal verification. We use an illustrative use case that consists of 6 processes,
allocated to 3 different CPMs that communicate with each other by means of a
switched network. These 6 processes exchange a total of 11 message types.

While a graphical representation of the architecture is depicted in Fig. 8, the
message graph of Fig. 9 shows the direction of each of the messages exchanged
by the processes, depicting the sender and receiver of each message. Figure 9
also outlines the message dependencies between processes, a fundamental piece
of information for the verification of Requirement 1. Listing 1.4, in turn, details
the declaration of each process and message, characterizing information such as
the period of the processes, the end-system each process is associated with, as
well as the size of each one of the 11 message types with each other.

The results of the verification of two different platform instantiations for
requirement 1 are shown in Table 1. The first instance considers that the network links of the candidate platform have a bandwidth of 1 Gbps; the second,
represents the case in which the network bandwidth is just 1 Mbps. Table 2, on
the other hand, shows the results of a verification of requirement 2, presenting
4 different instances of the platform with different buffer sizes for the network
models.

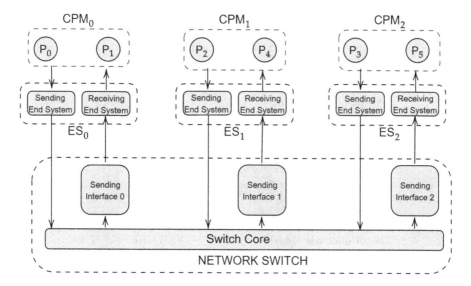

Fig. 8. Test case architecture

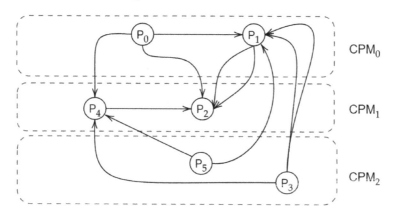

Fig. 9. Test case message graph

Analyzing the results obtained from the verification of requirement 1, it is easy to see that, whereas the instance featuring a fast network (1 Gbps bandwidth) was able to respect the communication deadlines imposed by the AAM, the instance featuring a slower network (1 Mbps bandwidth) did not meet this requirement. The result of this verification was already expected since this instance was created to illustrate, given the size of the messages, the bandwidth of the network, and the periodicity of the processes, how a bad choice of network bandwidth could lead to a breach of requirement 1.

Table 1. Requirement 1 verification results

Query: Req 1: Correct timing for data delivery		
Instance	Verification time (s)	Verification result
1 Gbps network	1868.05	SUCCESS
1 Mbps network	34.62	FAILURE

Table 2. Requirement 2 verification results

Query: Req 2: No messages dropped		
Instance	Verification time (s)	Verification result
8Kb Buffer size	3.29	FAILURE
16Kb Buffer size	3.36	FAILURE
32Kb Buffer size	16.04	FAILURE
64Kb Buffer size	1857.55	SUCCESS

Turning to the results in Table 2, the verification of requirement 2 leads to the conclusion that the components of the network should have buffers that are somewhere between 32 kb and 64 kb in size. This behavior can be explained by the periodicity of the processes. When the buffers are smaller than 32 kb the periodicity of the processes can lead to bursts of messages that small buffers cannot deal with.

The results also show that the verification approach performs quite well in cases in which the requirements are not met, being able to inform the user about resource inadequacy or network problems within seconds. When the system does not present any problem, however, the verification of the model takes considerably longer. This behaviour was already expected since proving that one of the requirements is not met is an easier task than proving that they are met. To prove that the requirements defined on Sect. 4 are met, the model-checker has to verify the whole state-space of the system to guarantee that no error state is ever reached. On the other hand, proving that the requirements are not met is as simple as finding one branch of the state-space of the system in which one of the error states is reached.

More importantly, the results from this case study show that the proposed approach suffers from a severe scalability problem. Experiments made with more processes and messages, such as 9 nodes and 16 messages, have shown a tendency of the model to quickly get into a state-explosion problem, using up too many computational resources and eventually leading the model-checker to terminate the verification with inconclusive results. Since a common IMA system can be composed of hundreds of processes, tenths of CPMs and end systems, and thousands of message classes, such behavior raises some concerns about the suitability of the system to be used in such cases.

```
// ----- processes
const Process processList[N_PROC]:={
{tid[0],7000,16000,esid[0], {3,{1,2,3}},    {0,{0,0,0,0}}},
{tid[1],6000,32000,esid[0], {2,{4,5,0}},    {4,{1,11,6,7}}},
{tid[2],3000,64000,esid[1], {0,{0,0,0}},    {4,{3,4,5,9}}},
{tid[3],5000,16000,esid[2], {3,{6,7,8}},    {0,{0,0,0,0}}},
{tid[4],8000,32000,esid[1], {1,{9,0,0}},    {3,{8,10,2,0}}},
{tid[5],3000,16000,esid[2], {2,{10,11,0}}, {0,{0,0,0,0}}}};

// ----- messages
const Message mList[N_MESS]:={
{0,1,1,3608},    {0,4,2,1449},    {0,2,3,8519},    {1,2,4,1519},
{1,2,5,145},     {3,1,6,10585},   {3,1,7,550},     {3,4,8,4956},
{4,2,9,3257},    {5,4,10,5674},   {5,1,11,391}};
```

Listing 1.4. Processes and Messages Declaration

6 Conclusions

This work has detailed the process and methods applied to the development and test of an integrated modular avionics platform performance evaluation model. The developed model was supposed to be a tool to help the professionals involved in the early conceptual phases of IMA architecture definition to evaluate and assess different architectures or platforms for their IMA system.

Through the verification of a candidate architecture, the model is shown to be capable of analyzing and verifying the network requirements of candidate architecture platforms. Such functionality, however, comes with a great cost in computational power and time even for small systems, showing an accentuated scalability problem with the current version of the model, something that can severely influence the usability of the solution. This leads us to the conclusion that, while the conceptual modelling approach developed in this work seems promising, the UPPAAL encoding of it does not seem to scale.

In conclusion, further work is needed to analyse real-life-sized IMA architectures of this nature. Moreover, extensions such as the addition of new message scheduling algorithms, creation of templates for different switches or network modules, and the support for different network standards and topologies could help to enrich the model and improve the value of the developed solution.

Acknowledgements. This work was supported by the Sweden's Innovation Agency - Vinnova, as part of the national projects on aeronautics, NFFP7, project CLASSICS (NFFP7-04890).

References

1. Robati, T., Gherbi, A., Mullins, J.: A modeling and verification approach to the design of distributed IMA architectures using TTEthernet. Procedia Comput. Sci. **83**, 229–236 (2016)
2. Alur, R., Dill, D.: Automata for modeling real-time systems. In: Paterson, M.S. (ed.) ICALP 1990. LNCS, vol. 443, pp. 322–335. Springer, Heidelberg (1990). https://doi.org/10.1007/BFb0032042
3. Cruz, R.L.: A calculus for network delay. I. Network elements in isolation. IEEE Trans. Inf. Theory **37**(1), 114–131 (1991)
4. Cruz, R.L.: A calculus for network delay. II. Network analysis. IEEE Trans. Inf. Theory **37**(1), 132–141 (1991)
5. Goldblatt, R.: Logics of Time and Computation, vol. 7. Center for the Study of Language and Information Stanford, California (1992)
6. Khaitan, S.K., McCalley, J.D.: Design techniques and applications of cyberphysical systems: a survey. IEEE Syst. J. **9**(2), 350–365 (2014)
7. Larsen, K.G., Pettersson, P., Yi, W.: UPPAAL in a nutshell. Int. J. Softw. Tools Technol. Trans. (STTT) **1**, 134–152 (1997)
8. Li, M., Zhu, G., Savaria, Y.: Delay bound analysis for heterogeneous multicore systems using network calculus. In: IEEE Conference on Industrial Electronics and Applications (ICIEA), pp. 1825–1830 (2018)
9. Soni, A., Li, X., Scharbarg, J., Fraboul, C.: Work in progress paper: pessimism analysis of network calculus approach on AFDX networks. In: IEEE International Symposium on Industrial Embedded Systems (SIES), pp. 1–4 (2017)
10. Wang, H., Niu, W.: A review on key technologies of the distributed integrated modular avionics system. Int. J. Wireless Inf. Networks **25**(3), 358–369 (2018)
11. Watkins, C.B.: Integrated modular avionics: managing the allocation of shared intersystem resources. In: IEEE/AIAA Digital Avionics Systems Conference, pp. 1–12 (2006)
12. Xu, Q., Yang, X.: Performance analysis on transmission estimation for avionics real-time system using optimized network calculus. Int. J. Aeronaut. Space Sci. **20**(2), 506–517 (2019)
13. Zhang, K., Wu, J., Liu, C., Ali, S.S., Ren, J.: Behavior modeling on ARINC653 to support the temporal verification of conformed application design. IEEE Access **7**, 23852–23863 (2019)

Automated Ada Code Generation from Synchronous Dataflow Programs on Multicore: Approach and Industrial Study

Shenghao Yuan[1]($\boxtimes$), Zhibin Yang[1]($\boxtimes$), Jean-Paul Bodeveix[2]($\boxtimes$),
Mamoun Filali[2]($\boxtimes$), Tiexin Wang[1]($\boxtimes$), and Yong Zhou[1]($\boxtimes$)

[1] College of Computer Science and Technology,
Nanjing University of Aeronautics and Astronautics, Nanjing, China
{shyuan,tiexin.wang,zhouyong}@nuaa.edu.cn, yangzhibin168@163.com
[2] IRIT, Université de Toulouse, Toulouse, France
{bodeveix,filali}@irit.fr

Abstract. The code synthesis, especially the multi-task code generation, plays an important role in the implementation of the safety-critical applications. MiniSIGNAL is a sequential/multi-task code generation tool for the synchronous language SIGNAL. During the application of real-world industrial case study, we find the generated programs is still inefficient due to a shortage of the original code generation strategies. Therefore, this paper presents a new multi-task code generation method for SIGNAL. Starting at the level of synchronous clocked guarded actions (S-CGA) which is an intermediate language for the compilation process of MiniSIGNAL, the transformation consists of two levels: At the platform-independent level, transforming the S-CGA code to an abstract multi-task structure (called VMT) with formal syntax and semantics; At the platform-dependent level, adopting the thread pool pattern to implement parallel Ada code generated from the VMT structure. The approach is applied to a real-world Guidance, Navigation and Control system to show the effectiveness of our approach.

Keywords: Safety-critical systems · Synchronous dataflow language · Multi-task code generation · Ada · Multi core

1 Introduction

Safety-Critical Systems (SCSs) are widely used in the fields of avionics, space systems, and nuclear power plants: Malfunctions of SCSs can lead to accidents that

Supported by organization by the National Natural Science Foundation of China (61502231); The National Key Research and Development Program of China (2016YFB1000802); The Natural Science Foundation of Jiangsu Province (BK20150753); The National Defense Basic Scientific Research Project under Grant of China (JCKY2016203B011); The Fundamental Research Funds for the Central Universities (NP2017205); the Foundation of Graduate Innovation Center in NUAA (kfjj20181603).

O. Hasan and F. Mallet (Eds.): FTSCS 2019, CCIS 1165, pp. 57–73, 2020.
https://doi.org/10.1007/978-3-030-46902-3_4

can potentially put people, environment, property, and mission in serious risks such as environmental catastrophes and loss of lives. Currently, Model-Driven Development (MDD) is generally accepted as a key enabler for the design of the SCSs. For example, MDD (DO-331) and formal methods (DO-333) are vital technology supplements which are added to extend the guide of DO-178C [9]. There are many MDD languages and approaches covering various modeling demands, such as UML for generic modeling, SysML for system-level modeling, AADL [8] for the architectural modeling and analysis of embedded systems, SCADE for synchronous dataflow modeling, Modelica for multi-domain modeling.

Synchronous languages, which rely on the synchronous hypothesis, are widely adopted in the design and verification of the SCSs. For example, Airbus has been using SCADE to develop the A380 Control and Display System [3]. There are several synchronous languages, such as ESTEREL [6], LUSTRE [17], QUARTZ [1] and SIGNAL [4]. As a main difference from other synchronous dataflow languages, SIGNAL is a kind of polychronous language (multi-clock), and it naturally considers a mathematical time model, in terms of a partial-order relation, to describe multi-clocked systems without the necessity of a global clock. With the advent of CPUs, it is a trend that multi-core CPUs will be widely used in the SCSs, so polychornous languages are more attractive for embedded designers.

In the multi-threaded code generation scheme, the existing SIGNAL compiler Polychrony [1][1] uses micro-level threading which creates a large number of threads and equally large number of semaphores, leading to inefficiency. In [18,19], we propose a novel multi-task code generator for SIGNAL, called MiniSIGNAL, which consists of the forth-end (from SIGNAL to Synchronous Clocked Guarded Action, S-CGA) and back-end (from S-CGA to target languages). The final purpose of MiniSIGNAL is to generate a new SIGNAL verified compiler in Coq.

When the existing MiniSIGNAL code strategies are applied for the industrial case study, the execution efficiency of generated multi-task program is not satisfactory because frequent task switching costs a lot (saving all registers, moving tasks into the ready queue, reloading new tasks and updating stack data from memory, etc.) in a multi-task environment, especially when the number of CPUs is small. To generate more efficient target code from industrial cases, this paper presents a new multi-task code generation method based on MiniSIGNAL. This paper selects Ada as the target language because Ada is an explicit-concurrency and high-safety programming language which is very popular in the SCSs, especially in the Chinese aerospace industrial field. In addition, this paper compares the proposed approach to some closely related works (e.g. Schneider [1]) discussed later in order to provide more empirical evidence about the usefulness of our approach and the existing works when applied in industrial settings. The main contributions presented in the paper can be summarized as follows:

- A new approach is proposed for transforming S-CGA models to multi-task Ada code. The transformation is divided into two parts:

---

[1] http://www.irisa.fr/espresso/Polychrony/.

- Platform-independent level. A platform-independent structure, called Virtual Multi-Task (VMT), is defined as a common multi-task structure to explicitly express concurrency information, its syntax and semantics are shown in Coq. The transformation algorithm from S-CGA to VMT is also shown in Sect. 3.
- Platform-dependent level. The thread pool pattern is adopted for implementing the platform-dependent parallel code. The algorithm is given about transforming VMT structures to multi-task Ada code.

- A real-world aerospace industrial case, the Guidance, Navigation and Control (GNC) system, is used to show the feasibility of the method presented in the paper. This paper mainly shows three subsystems of GNC which are suitable for modeling in SIGNAL: Attitude Determination subsystem, Orbit Calculation subsystem and Attitude Control subsystem. The subsystems are also used for strategies comparisons to indicate the effectiveness of various code generation strategies when applied to industrial cases.

The rest of this paper is organized as follows. Section 2 briefly introduces SIGNAL and S-CGA. Section 3 presents a multi-task Ada code generation approach which includes the platform-independent level and the platform-dependent level. Section 4 gives a real-world aerospace industrial case study. Section 5 gives some lessons learnt and discussions. Section 6 discusses some related works and Sect. 7 provides concluding remarks and plans for future work.

2 Preliminary

In this section, we first introduce some basic concepts of SIGNAL, and then give the definition of the intermediate format S-CGA.

2.1 SIGNAL

As declared in the synchronous hypothesis, the behaviors of a reactive system are divided into a discrete sequence of instants. At each instant, the system does input-computation-output, which takes zero time. So a variable (called *signal*) in SIGNAL is an infinite sequence, at each instant, a signal may be present with a value or absent (denoted by $\perp$). The set of instants where a signal x takes a value is the abstract clock (denoted by $\hat{x}$). Two signals are synchronous if they are always present and absent at the same instants, which means they have the same abstract clock.

SIGNAL provides four primitive constructs to express the relations between signals:

- instantaneous function $y := f(x_1, x_2, \ldots, x_n)$
- delay $y := x \; \$ \; init \; c$
- undersampling $y := x \; when \; b$
- deterministic merging $y := x_1 \; default \; x_2$

The instantaneous function and the delay are *monoclock* operators which mean all signals involved have the same abstract clock, while the undersampling and the deterministic merging are *multiclock* operators which mean the signals involved may have different clocks.

SIGNAL also provides some extended constructs to express control-relate properties by specifying clock relations explicitly, for example set operators on clocks (union $x_1\char"5E+x_2$, intersection $x_1\char"5E*x_2$, difference $x_1\char"5E-x_2$). But each extended construct is equivalent to a set of primitive constructs.

In the SIGNAL language, the relations between values and the relations between abstract clocks, of the signals, are defined as equations, and a *process* consists of a set of equations. Two basic operators apply to processes, the first one is the *composition* of different processes, and the other one is the *local declaration* in which the scope of a signal is restricted to a process.

2.2   S-CGA

We present the intermediate representation called S-CGA which is proposed in the MiniSIGNAL code generator.

Definition 1 (S-CGA). An S-CGA system is a set of guarded actions $\langle \gamma \Rightarrow \mathcal{A} \rangle$ defined over a set of variables X. The Boolean condition γ is called the guard and $\mathcal{A}$ is called the action. Intuitively, the semantics of guarded actions is that $\mathcal{A}$ is executed if γ holds. Guarded actions can be of one of the following forms:

(1) $\gamma \Rightarrow x = \tau$ (*immediate*)

(2) $\gamma \Rightarrow next\,(x) = \tau$ (*delayed*)

(3) $\gamma \Rightarrow assume\,(\sigma)$ (*assumption*)

(4) $\gamma \Rightarrow read\,(x)$ (*input*)

(5) $\gamma \Rightarrow write\,(x)$ (*output*)

where,

- γ and σ are Boolean conditions over the variables of X, and their clocks. For a variable $x \in X$, we denote:
  - its clock $\widehat{x}$,
  - its initial clock $init(\widehat{x})$ as the clock which ticks the first time (if any) where $\widehat{x}$ ticks.
- τ is an expression over X

The form (1) immediately writes the value of τ to the variable x. The form (2) evaluates τ in the given instant but changes the value of the variable x at its next instant of presence. The form (3) defines a constraint which has to hold when γ is defined and true. The form (4) shows x that gets a value provided by the environment while the form (5) indicates the environment gets a value x if γ is defined and true. Guarded actions are composed by the parallel operator $\|$.

3   Ada Code Generation Approach

Based on the existing front-end of MiniSIGNAL, the new Ada code generation process is shown in Fig. 1, which adds two parts: Virtual Multi-Task generation (platform-independent) and Multi-task Ada generation (platform-dependent). The Virtual Multi-Task is defined for explicitly expressing synchronization relations derived from SIGNAL. Synchronization relations are implemented between the tasks of VMT using the Wait/Notify mechanism. Such an abstract structure is expected to support some purposes, such as generating simulation code (e.g. Simulink), formal verification model (e.g. UPPAAL) and various target executable code (e.g. C/Java/Ada) from VMT.

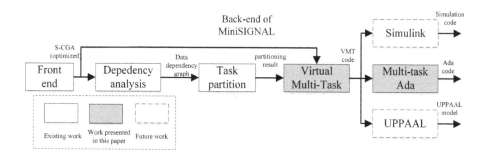

Fig. 1. Multi-task Ada code generation.

3.1   Dependency Analysis and Task Partition

Dependency Analysis. The guarded actions have to be executed in data flow order to avoid the read-after-write conflicts, so Data Dependency Graph (DDG) should be constructed. DDG is a directed acyclic graph consisting of vertices representing guarded actions and edges representing the dependencies between the actions. The edge $\gamma_1 \Rightarrow \mathcal{A}_1 \rightarrow \gamma_2 \Rightarrow \mathcal{A}_2$ expresses there exists a variable x such that x occurs in the left-hand side of action $\mathcal{A}_1$ and also occurs in the guard γ_2 or in the right-hand side of action $\mathcal{A}_2$.

Task Partition. There are different partition methods, such as the topological sorting way [11], the vertical way [1] and the horizontal way [2]. Here we select a more general way: The main idea is to map the guarded actions to tasks in the target languages one by one, and to convert the read/write dependencies to the synchronous communication between tasks.

3.2   Platform-Independent Level: VMT Generation

VMT Syntax. VMT defines a set of sequential behaviors called tasks. After a global synchronization, tasks are fired according to the wait/notify mechanism.

When all tasks have completed their tasks, the state of the system is updated and an iteration is performed.

Definition 2 (Virtual Multi-Task (VMT)). A VMT structure is a tuple ⟨**Task**, **Init**, **Next**⟩, where,

- **Task** is a set of tasks (defined in the next paragraph).
- **Init** is an assignment action which assigns initial values to global variables before the first run of all the tasks.
- **Next** is an action that updates the global variables after each iteration.

The VMT structure is defined in Coq. *taskId* is the set of task identifiers. *tasks* associates a task definition to a *taskId*.

```
Structure VMT := {
  taskId: Type; (* set of task identifiers *)
  State: Type; (* internal state of the system *)
  Init: State; (* initial state of a task *)
  Next: State -> State;
  tasks: taskId -> Task taskId State }.
```

A task *tk* is a tuple ⟨**Id**, **Wait**, **Cond**, **Comp**, **Notify**⟩ where,

- **Id**: a String representing the identification of the task *tk*, such as T1.
- **Wait**: a set of tasks'**Id**, of which notification is waited for by *tk* before starting its execution. *tk* is fired if all tasks waited by *tk* has been executed.
- **Cond**: a Boolean condition expression. If the expression is true then the statement in Comp can be executed, otherwise the statement is skipped.
- **Comp**: a sequential statement including *input*, *computation* or *output*.
- **Notify**: a set of tasks'**Id** that must be notified once *tk* has been executed. **Wait** and **Notify** can be used to synchronize tasks.

The Coq definition of a task is shown below, where **Cond** is represented as a predicate over the state, and **Comp** as a function from state to state.

```
Structure Task Id State:= {
  Wait: Ensemble Id;
  Cond: State -> Prop;
  Comp: forall st: State, Guard st -> State;
  Notify: Ensemble Id; }.
```

VMT Semantics. The semantics of a VMT is defined by a transition system (TS) which is a pair ⟨S, →⟩ where S is a set of states and →⊆ $S \times S$ is a set of state transitions. In order to give the semantics of a VMT, we first need to define its state. It contains three parts:

- vmState: the user state as introduced in the VMT, which is shared and updated by all the tasks;
- ctState: the control state of each task, which takes three values: *csWait*, *csReady* and *csEnd*;
- notified: the set of notifications currently received.

The Coq representation expresses the structure of transition systems and inductively defines four kinds of transitions:

- *TrWait*(id): if *id* is in *csWait* and the set of waited tasks of *id* is included in its notified set, *id* goes to *csReady*.
- *TrComp*(id): if *id* is in *csReady* and its condition is satisfied, its action is executed updating the VMT state, notifications are sent and *id* goes to *csEnd*.
- *TrNoComp*(id): if *id* is in *csReady* and its condition is not satisfied, notifications are sent and *id* goes to *csEnd*.
- *TrNext*(id): if all tasks are in *csReady*, they are all put in *csWait* and the Next VMT transition is executed.

Finally, the semantics of VMT as a TS is defined in Coq by a one-to-one mapping. For more details, please referring to https://github.com/nuaaysh/VMTinCoq/blob/master/VMT.v.

```
Structure TS := {
  LState:  Type;
  LInit:  LState;
  LTrans:  LState -> LState -> Prop }.
Inductive trans (vmt:VMT) (st1:  state vmt) (st2:  state vmt):  Prop :=
  trWait:  forall id , TrWait vmt st1 st2 id -> trans vmt st1 st2
  | trComp:  forall id , TrComp vmt st1 st2 id -> trans vmt st1 st2
  | trNoComp:  forall id , TrNoComp vmt st1 st2 id -> trans vmt st1 st2
  | trNext:  TrNext vmt st1 st2 -> trans vmt st1 st2.
Definition VMT2TS (vmt:  VMT) := {|
  LState := state vmt;
  LInit := mk_state _ (Init vmt) (fun _ => csWait) (fun _ => Empty_set _);
  LTrans := trans vmt |}.
```

Remark: The purpose of the introduction of VMT is not to define a new language but to provide a common multi-tasking structure used as a target for the compilation of synchronous languages. Thus, we do not show the coq representations of some concepts (such as variables, data type and data structure) which are derived from the source SIGNAL specifications.

S-CGA2VMT. VMT can be structurally translated from S-CGA and DDG by generating each element separately, as shown in Algorithm 1. The algorithm first generates the **Init** field by the initial clock of S-CGA (line 02) and the **Next** field by the delay actions (line 03). Each task is then produced from vertices of the DDG (line 04–line 16): For each vertex (i.e. a guarded action), the corresponding task'**Id** depends on the place where the guarded action appears in S-CGA specifications (line 05); the **Guard** field is generated from the guard of the guarded action (line 06); the **Comp** field is generated from the action of the guarded action (line 07); the **Wait** and **Notify** are generated according to two rules: For each edge whose ending vertex is the current vertex, their starting vertices are added to the **Wait** (line 09–line 10); Likewise, for each edge whose starting vertex is the current vertex, their ending vertices are added to the **Notify** (line 11–line 12). Then the generated task is added to the **Task** field of VMT (line 15). In addition, the algorithm implicitly includes the idea of the task partition method.

3.3   Platform-Dependent Level: Ada Code Generation

There are quite easy ways to generate multi-task Ada code. For example, we could associate one Ada task to each DDG node and use the Ada *rendezvous mechanism* or protected objects to control race conditions. However, the generated code would be inefficient as it would contain too many tasks. Therefore, in this section, we have chosen another way to generate Ada code.

Algorithm 1. S-CGA2VMT.

Input: $S - CGA, DDG$
Output: $genVMT$
1: **procedure** gen_VMT:
2:    $genVMT.Init \leftarrow$ getInit$(S - CGA)$; //Init
3:    $genVMT.Next \leftarrow$ getNext$(S - CGA)$; //Next
4:    **For each** $v_i \in DDG$ **do** //Task
5:      $t_i.Id \leftarrow$ getId(DDG, v_i);
6:      $t_i.Guard \leftarrow$ getGuard(DDG, v_i);
7:      $t_i.Comp \leftarrow$ getComp(DDG, v_i);
8:      **For each** $e_j \in DDG$ **do** //Task
9:        **If** $e_j.end\_vertex() = v_i$ **then**
10:          $t_i.Wait \leftarrow$ addWait$(e_j.start\_vertex())$;
11:        **Else If** $e_j.start\_vertex() = v_i$ **then**
12:          $t_i.Notify \leftarrow$ addNotify$(e_j.end\_vertex)$;
13:        **end If**
14:      **end For**
15:      $genVMT.Task \leftarrow$ addTask(t_i);
16:    **end For**
17:    **return** $genVMT$;
18: **end procedure**

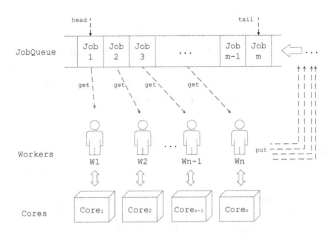

Fig. 2. JobQueue-Workers.

We have chosen the thread pool pattern to implement the parallel computation of DDG (Fig. 2): a JobQueue that stores all ready jobs (i.e. procedures in Ada), and workers that get jobs from the head of the queue and execute them in parallel on separate cores. After one jobs is completed, all waiting jobs that depend on the job are put in the tail of the queue by the related worker.

Following the code generation principle [4]. The top-level structure of generated Ada code is an infinite loop of elementary iterations: the *main* program calls the *init* function, then keeps calling the *tasks* function. Once the *tasks* function is completed, the *next* function is called before next calling the *tasks* function.

We first define a JobQueue protected type offering two operations: *put* and *get* which allow adding a ask to the queue and extracting a job to the queue provided it is not empty. Concurrent calls to these entries will be sequentialized by the protected object.

```
type job is access procedure;
type index is mod M; -- M is the size of the queue
type todolist is array (index) of job;
protected JobQueue is
     entry put(a:in job);
     entry get(a:out job);
   private
     todo  : todolist := (others => null);
     head  : index := 0;
     tail  : index := 0;
     count : integer range 0..M := 0;
end JobQueue;
```

A worker is bound to a specific CPU and makes an infinite loop: extracting a job from the queue and executing it.

```
task type worker (N : CPU_Range) with CPU => N is
end worker;
task body worker is
     a:job;
begin
     loop
          JobQueue.get(a);
          a.all;
     end loop;
end worker;
worker1 : worker(1);
...
```

To implement the Wait/Notify mechanism, a counter should be defined with a protected type. each job has one counter with an initial value, which is the number of jobs it depends on. When one of them is completed, the value decreases by 1 (i.e. calling the procedure *decr* once). If the return value of *decr* is true, then the job can be executed.

```
protected type counter(init: integer := 1) is
     procedure decr(z: out boolean);
   private
     c:integer := init;
end counter;
```

The other transformations from VMT to Ada are trivial: The *init* function generated from **Init** is defined in the program body of the *main*, each task of VMT is mapped to a procedure (or job). The procedure *next* generated from **Next** is fired when all jobs have already been completed. It updates memory for the next time step.

```
c_next : counter(5); -- wait the five terminal jobs
procedure next is
      rdy : boolean;
begin
      c_next.decr(rdy);
      if (not rdy) then return; end if;
      -- next field: update memory for next time step
      -- restart running
      JobQueue.put(t01'Access);
      --t02.. t15
      JobQueue.put(t16'Access);
      end if;
end next;
-- Main procedure
begin
      -- init function: initialize memory
      -- start running
      JobQueue.put(t01'Access);
      --t02.. t15
      JobQueue.put(t16'Access);
end Main;
```

4   Industrial Case Study

The Guidance, Navigation and Control (GNC) system is a core system supporting orbiting operations of spacecrafts, which undertakes the tasks of determining
and controlling spacecraft attitude and orbit. For such a complex embedded system, we use AADL to model the complex hierarchical architecture of GNC, adopt
AADL Behavior Annex to describe the components involved many control flow
information, and use SIGNAL model to express the components involving a large
amount of dataflow computation. SIGNAL models are encapsulated in AADL
models by using the AADL extension mechanism based on property sets. In this
paper, we select three subsystems involved SIGNAL models as study cases.

- CASE_A: Data Processing of Sun Sensor. The subsystem mainly performs
  the computation about data processing according to the data received from
  sun sensors.
- CASE_B: Computation of Orbit Elements. The subsystem is used to derive
  orbital elements at a particular time according to the system clock and the
  GPS data.
- CASE_C: Eliminate Initial Deviation. The subsystem eliminates the angular
  rate of attitude generated by the separation of satellites from launch vehicles
  by calling some three-axis attitude control algorithms of spacecraft.

Table 1. Statistical data of generated code of three cases.

Case	Task number	Synchronous communication (Number of dependencies edge)	Size of Ada code (line)
CASE_A	66	71	1200+
CASE_B	56	84	1100+
CASE_C	25	35	700+

The statistical data of Ada code generation (three cases) is shown in Table 1. In particular, the Ada code generation method is illustrated by the CASE_A.

4.1 Code Generation of Data Processing of Sun Sensor

The CASE_A involves two kinds hardware devices: Three sun sensors of the Satellite (Sa, Sb, Sc) and a sun sensor of the Solar Array (SA), each sun sensor has four batteries. The CASE_A receives the input data from the hardware devices, performs the data processing (including 4 natural parallel sub-processes) and sends the results to other subsystems (e.g. Data Processing of Star Sensor).

The main requirement of CASE_A consists of:

- **Req1.1**: Converting the source code of the sensors (Sa, Sb, Sc) to the corresponding voltage value.
- **Req1.2**: Computing the voltage value of four batteries of each sensor, if a sensor doesn't satisfy the related constraint, resetting the solar angle to zero, otherwise calculating the solar angle.
- **Req1.3**: Computing the filter of each solar angle by the filter algorithms.
- **Req1.4**: Using the data from two sensors (Sb and Sc) to calculate the projection of the sun vector in the satellite celestial coordinate system.
- **Req2.1**: Converting the source code of the sensor (SA) to the corresponding voltage value.
- **Req2.2**: Calculating the solar angle of the solar array.
- **Req2.3**: Computing the filter of the solar angle.

Figure 3 illustrates the process of translating synchronous specifications to multi-task Ada code. Starting with the set of guarded actions generation by the MiniSIGNAL tool (a), the data dependency graph (b) is constructed by the read/write dependencies. Following the transformation algorithm, the VMT structure (c) is generated from the S-CGA code and the graph. Finally, The generated Ada code (e.g. task36) is shown in (d).

4.2 Strategies Comparisons

The main purpose of the multi-core experiment is that compares the execution time of generated Ada programs using different code generation strategies:

- seq (benchmark): Sequential code generation from MiniSIGNAL.
- basic: Multi-task code generation from the original MiniSIGNAL (Semaphores).
- jobqueue: Multi-task code using thread pool pattern mentioned in this paper.
- Schneider: Multi-task code using the vertical task partition method [1].

The strategies *seq* and *basic* are proposed in the [18] and [19]. The link (https://github.com/nuaaysh/vSIGNAL/tree/master/Example/GNC/Schneid er) explains the *Schneider*'s code generation strategy using the CASE_A.

The experiment environment includes: windows 10 64-bit operation system, 8-cores i7-7700 CPU 3.600 GHz, 16G RAM, Ada2012 and the IDE of Ada (GPS

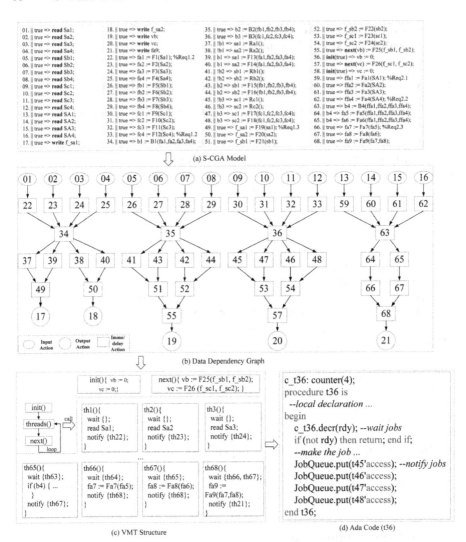

Fig. 3. The transformation process from S-CGA to Ada (CASE_A).

6.2). The benchmark is the execution result of the sequential Ada code generated from MiniSIGNAL. Furthermore, the number of CPUs is statically set to 1, 2, 4 and 8, respectively.

Figure 4 shows the experiment results of the three GNC subsystems (CASE_-A/B/C). In the figure, the abscissa is the number of CPUs, the ordinate is the execution time (the average value of executing 1000 times). The average time shows the execution efficiency of generated Ada code using different generation strategies. For same number of CPUs, the efficiency of the jobqueue-style Ada code is best, followed by the Schneider'method. The original MiniSIGNAL strategy is inefficient because it produces lots of task switching which may take much time to save registers, reload stack from memory, etc. And the jobqueue-style is efficient because tasks of VMT are mapped to jobs and Ada tasks are created once for all and mapped to cores, there is no task switch as a core always runs its tasks. In addition, when there is only one/two CPUs, the results of original/Schneider's method are even worse than the one of the sequential method, a potential reason is that the complex task communication leads to some 'conflicts' within one CPU (or between two CPUs).

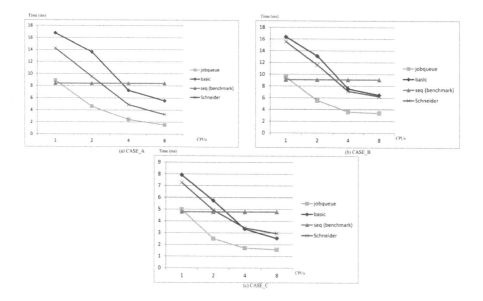

Fig. 4. The experiment results of CASE_A/B/C on multi-core

In summary, the following conclusions are drawn from the experimentations:

- Given a code generation strategy(except the sequential one), there is a positive correlation between the CPUs' number and the execution efficiency.
- The jobqueue-style strategy significantly improves the execution efficiency of the target program (comparing with the other two strategies).

4.3 Threat to Validity

To reduce possible threat on validity, we communicated with industry partners iteratively to obtain more information and tried to make the case more real. Even though, we still find some internal and external factors that may influence the validity of the Ada code generation approach for SIGNAL.

- *Internal Threat.* The code style is a potential factor to affect the execution efficiency of generated programs, for example, too many global variables presented in the computation of tasks procedure a lot of shared-memory accesses.

A solution is that each task declares some local variables which are used to replace the occurs of the global variables. Each modified task does Input (assigning the values of the global variables to the corresponding local variables) - Computation (performing the computation only using local variables) - Output (assigning the values of the local variables to the corresponding global variables).

It is interesting to remark that although the concurrency pattern we have used is basically the "producer-consumer" one, we have to be careful with respect to the size of the buffer. Actually, if the buffer size is too small, the following deadlock can occur: all busy workers cannot terminate because the buffer is currently full and consequently cannot release their currently held slot. In order to avoid such a situation, the buffer should be sized at least to the width of the underlying dependency relation partial order.

- *External Threat.* The efficiency of multi-task Ada code generation method for SIGNAL also depends on selected systems. In fact, we find the method is suitable for the radar subsystem and GNC, because these systems naturally contain many parallel computation (e.g. the radar subsystem has many modules to capture different objects), while the multi-core experiment results aren't very well when considering the rocket launch control subsystem because the subsystem has too much synchronous communication between tasks. Therefore, a system with less synchronous communication consumption is better for using the method mentioned in the paper.

5   Lessons Learnt and Discussions

During the collaboration with our industrial partner for devising the methodology and conducting the industrial case study, we learned the following lessons and identified some challenges when applying the multi-task Ada code generation methodology in real industrial contexts.

In the safety-critical domain, a number of standards (e.g. DO-178B/C for avionics, ISO 26262 for automotive systems and CENELEC EN 50128 for railway systems, etc.) are recommended to be followed when using MDD languages/approaches to develop the safety-critical systems/software and many MDD languages and approaches. In particular, Chinese aerospace industry is accustomed to constructing complex embedded systems with different levels of modeling languages, such as using SysML to construct system-level information, adopting AADL to model architectural information and using Synchronous languages (e.g. SCADE) to expressing platform-independent functional information, etc. In addition, our industry partners pay more attention on the multi-task code generation methods involved these modeling languages, because the computation performance of mutli-core is quite attractive for their embedded designers.

Although we use a basic task partition method in the paper, our method can be adopted for a multi-task code generation framework to integrate more task partition methods or optimization strategies for the purpose of higher efficiency. For example, the optimized results using a merging partitions' strategy [19] (opt) is better than the one without optimization (no_opt) in Table 2. We are carrying out research about the framework, some special methods/strategies may request some modifications of VMT, for example, an additional structure may be necessary to express the *pipeline mechanism* when integrating the horizontal partition method [2].

Table 2. The results of the original (no_opt)/optimized (opt) program for three cases.

CASE	Category	Task number	Synchronous communication	Execution time (ms)			
				1-cores	2-cores	4-cores	8-cores
CASE_A	no_opt	66	71	8.90	4.60	2.40	1.52
	opt	45	50	8.76	4.56	2.35	1.51
CASE_B	no_opt	56	84	9.51	5.55	3.58	3.37
	opt	44	72	9.47	5.42	3.48	3.21
CASE_C	no_opt	25	35	4.97	2.51	1.70	1.56
	opt	21	31	4.97	2.51	1.68	1.49

6   Related Work

Many tools/compilers for synchronous languages have been proposed to design the safety-critical applications, such as Esterelv5_92[2] for generating C-code or hardware from Esterel code, SCADE for generating C/Ada-code from Lustre specifications, Averest[3] for generating C/Java/SystemC/VHDL-code from Quartz programs, and Polychrony for generating C/Java from Signal code. With the advent of multi-core processors, automated synthesis of multi-threaded code from synchronous models has gradually become a hotspot of research.

Baudisch et al. [1,2] propose two synthesis procedures generating multi-threaded OpenMP-based C code from QUARTZ by vertical/horizontal partitioning respectively.

Krebs et al. [13] provide a framework to convert RVC-CAL (a dataflow language) specification to SYCL or OpenCL based code, which supports to parallelise both synchronous and non-synchronous dataflow. In [15], they also considers both the coarse-grained (task-parallel) execution of actors using multithreading and the fine-grained (data-parallel) execution of their actions using SYCL or OpenCL.

Colaço et al. [7] present an approach that first generates a Kaph process network (KPN) from SCADE models with annotations that no not affect the semantics but tells the compiler to generate independent tasks and then generates a target-specific code.

Giannopoulou et al. [10] propose a design flow covering specification to correct-by-construction implementation for mixed-criticality systems running on the Kalray MPPA®-256 many-core platform.

---

[2] http://www-sop.inria.fr/esterel.org/files/Html/Downloads/Downloads.htm.
[3] http://www.averest.org/.

Souyris et al. [17] propose the solutions for automatic parallel code generation from Lustre/Heptagon models with no-functional specification (e.g. period).

Li et al. [14] present the transformation from SystemJ code to implementation on two types of time-predictable cores, the evolutionary algorithm is used to evaluate multi-core scheduling solution for finding guaranteed reaction time of real-time synchronous programs for multi-core targets.

In terms of multi-threaded code generation for SIGNAL, the report [4] describes multi-threaded code generation strategies available in the Polychrony toolset, including clustered code generation with static and dynamic scheduling, distributed code generation. Jose et al. [12] propose a process-oriented and non-invasive multi-threaded code generation using the sequential code generators in Polychrony and separately synthesize some programming glue. Our previous works [18,19] present a sequential/multi-task C/Java code generator for SIGNAL. Comparing with [18,19], this paper focuses on improving the efficiency of target code when applied to real-world aerospace industrial cases.

7   Conclusion and Future Work

Synchronous languages are widely adopted for the design and verification of SCSs. With the advent of multi-core processors, multi-task code generation for synchronous languages has become a trend. MiniSIGNAL is a code generation tool for SIGNAL, which supports both sequential and multi-task target code. However the generated code is still inefficient when we apply the tool to the real-world aerospace industrial cases. Therefore, this paper presents a new method for generating multi-task jobqueue-style Ada code from synchronous specifications. Our method first generates a platform-independent multi-task structure (VMT) from S-CGA models, then generates target Ada code with the jobqueue pattern from VMT. The industrial case study has shown that the approach is feasible.

For future work, we would like to integrate more multi-task code generation strategies (e.g. [2,7] and [13]) in order to provide more empirical evidence about some interesting topics like the usefulness and the effectiveness when applied to real-world industrial applications. In addition, the adoption of automatic code generation techniques for safety-critical applications requires the formal verification of the approach. For example, two research teams (Vélus [5] and L2C [16]) are carrying out the verified sequential compilation of Lustre in Coq, respectively. We are currently working on the proof of semantics preservation of MiniSIGNAL, the verification details of the whole code generator will be the subject of a future communication.

References

1. Baudisch, D., Brandt, J., Schneider, K.: Multithreaded code from synchronous programs: extracting independent threads for OpenMP. In: Design, Automation & Test in Europe Conference & Exhibition (DATE 2010), pp. 949–952. IEEE (2010)

2. Baudisch, D., Brandt, J., Schneider, K.: Multithreaded code from synchronous programs: generating software pipelines for OpenMP. In: MBMV, pp. 11–20 (2010)
3. Berry, G.: Synchronous design and verification of critical embedded systems using SCADE and Esterel. In: Leue, S., Merino, P. (eds.) FMICS 2007. LNCS, vol. 4916, p. 2. Springer, Heidelberg (2008). https://doi.org/10.1007/978-3-540-79707-4_2
4. Besnard, L., Gautier, T., Talpin, J.P.: Code generation strategies in the Polychrony environment. Research Report RR-6894, INRIA (2009)
5. Bourke, T., Brun, L., Dagand, P.E., Leroy, X., Pouzet, M., Rieg, L.: A formally verified compiler for Lustre. In: 38th ACM SIGPLAN Conference on Programming Language Design and Implementation, Barcelone, Spain. ACM, June 2017
6. Boussinot, F., De Simone, R.: The ESTEREL language. Proc. IEEE **79**(9), 1293–1304 (1991)
7. Colaço, J.L., Pagano, B., Pasteur, C., Pouzet, M.: Scade 6: from a Kahn semantics to a Kahn implementation for multicore. In: 2018 Forum on Specification & Design Languages (FDL), pp. 5–16. IEEE (2018)
8. Feiler, P.H., Gluch, D.P.: Model-Based Engineering with AADL: An Introduction to the SAE Architecture Analysis & Design Language. Pearson Schweiz AG, Zug (2013)
9. Ferrell, T.K., Ferrell, U.D.: RTCA DO-178C/EUROCAE ED-12C. In: Digital Avionics Handbook (2017)
10. Giannopoulou, G., et al.: DOL-BIP-Critical: a tool chain for rigorous design and implementation of mixed-criticality multi-core systems. Des. Autom. Embed. Syst. **22**(1), 141–181 (2018). https://doi.org/10.1007/s10617-018-9206-3
11. Hu, K., Zhang, T., Shang, L., Yang, Z., Talpin, J.P.: Parallel code generation from synchronous specification. J. Softw. **28**, 1–15 (2017)
12. Jose, B.A., Patel, H.D., Shukla, S.K., Talpin, J.P.: Generating multi-threaded code from polychronous specifications. Electron. Notes Theor. Comput. Sci. **238**(1), 57–69 (2009)
13. Krebs, F.: A translation framework from RVC-CAL dataflow programs to Open-CL/SYCL based implementations. Master's thesis, Department of Computer Science, University of Kaiserslautern, Germany, January 2019
14. Li, Z., et al.: Using design space exploration for finding schedules with guaranteed reaction times of synchronous programs on multi-core architecture. J. Syst. Architect. **74**, 30–45 (2017)
15. Rafique, O., Krebs, F., Schneider, K.: Generating efficient parallel code from the RVC-CAL dataflow language. In: Euromicro Conference on Digital System Design (DSD), Kallithea, Chalkidiki, Greece. IEEE Computer Society (2019)
16. Shi, G., Zhang, Y., Shang, S., Wang, S., Dong, Y., Yew, P.C.: A formally verified transformation to unify multiple nested clocks for a lustre-like language. Sci. China Inf. Sci. **62**(1), 12801 (2019)
17. Souyris, J., et al.: Automatic parallelization from Lustre models in avionics. In: ERTS2 2018-9th European Congress Embedded Real-Time Software and Systems, pp. 1–4 (2018)
18. Yang, Z., Bodeveix, J.P., Filali, M.: Towards a simple and safe Objective Caml compiling framework for the synchronous language SIGNAL. Front. Comput. Sci. **13**(4), 715–734 (2019). https://doi.org/10.1007/s11704-017-6485-y
19. Yang, Z., Bodeveix, J.P., Filali, M., Hu, K., Zhao, Y., Ma, D.: Towards a verified compiler prototype for the synchronous language SIGNAL. Front. Comput. Sci. **10**(1), 37–53 (2016). https://doi.org/10.1007/s11704-015-4364-y

Applications

POP: A Tuning Assistant
for Mixed-Precision Floating-Point
Computations

Dorra Ben Khalifa[1]([✉]), Matthieu Martel[1,2], and Assalé Adjé[1]

[1] LAMPS Laboratory, University of Perpignan, 52 Av. P. Alduy, Perpignan, France
{dorra.ben-khalifa,matthieu.martel,assale.adje}@univ-perp.fr
[2] Numalis, Cap Omega, Rond-point Benjamin Franklin, Montpellier, France

Abstract. In this article, we describe a static program analysis to determine the lowest floating-point precisions on inputs and intermediate results that guarantees a desired accuracy of the output values. A common practice used by developers without advanced training in computer arithmetic consists in using the highest precision available in hardware (double precision on most CPU's) which can be exorbitant in terms of energy consumption, memory traffic, and bandwidth capacity. To overcome this difficulty, we propose a new precision tuning tool for the floating-point programs integrating a static forward and backward analysis, done by abstract interpretation. Next, our analysis will be expressed as a set of linear constraints easily checked by an SMT solver.

Keywords: Floating-point arithmetic · Mixed precision · Forward and backward error analysis · Constraints generation · SMT solver

1 Introduction

With the wide availability of processors with hardware floating-point units, many current critical applications, such as the critical control command systems for automotive, aeronautic, space, etc., which have stringent correctness requirements and whose failures have catastrophic consequences that endanger human life [1,9], rely heavily on floating-point operations. Without any extensive background in numerical accuracy and computer arithmetic, developers tend to use the highest precision available in hardware (usually double precision). Despite the fact that the results will be more accurate, this increases significantly the application runtime, bandwidth capacity and the memory and energy consumption of the system. In fact, we denote by the term *precision* the amount of information used to represent a value while the term *accuracy* denotes how close a floating-point computation comes to the real value. The challenge is to use no more precision than needed wherever possible without compromising overall accuracy (using a too low precision for a given algorithm and data set leads to inaccurate results). To overcome the problem of determining the accuracy of floating-point computations, many efforts have been done in automating

© Springer Nature Switzerland AG 2020
O. Hasan and F. Mallet (Eds.): FTSCS 2019, CCIS 1165, pp. 77–94, 2020.
https://doi.org/10.1007/978-3-030-46902-3_5

the choice of the best precision by dynamic or static methods [5,10,15,16] but they differ strongly in their way of accuracy determination. In this article, we are interested in the problem of determining the minimal precision on the inputs and the intermediary results of a program performing floating-point computations in order to get a desired accuracy on the outputs. Often in these programs, it is possible to reduce the floating-point precision of certain variables in order to increase performance, for example, the throughput of single-precision floating-point operations is twice that of double-precision operations. Also, the proposed tool in this article aims to apply the mixed-precision on the floating-point programs formats. Mixed-precision computing [10] is an approach to combine different precisions for different floating-point variables (contrarily to the uniform precision). Our approach combines a forward and a backward error analysis which are two popular paradigms of error analysis, done by abstract interpretations [3]. In fact, the forward analysis is classical. It examines how errors are magnified by each operation aiming to determine the accuracy on the results [11]. Next, a user requirement is given denoting the final accuracy wanted on some control points of the outputs. By taking in consideration the user assertions and the results of the forward analysis, the backward analysis is a complementary approach that starts with the computed answer to determine the exact floating-point input that would produce it in order to satisfy the desired accuracy. As could be expected, the forward and backward analysis can be handled iteratively to refine the results until a fixed-point is reached. Next, these forward and backward transfer functions are expressed as a set of linear constraints made of propositional logic formulas and relations between integer elements only. After, these constraints will be easily checked by an SMT solver (Z3 is used in practice [7]).

The main contributions of this article are the following. First, we introduce refinements of the automated approach based on a static forward and backward analysis done in [11]. This approach will be explained in details specially for the cases of addition, the multiplication and the subtraction arithmetic expressions. Furthermore, our contribution revolves around the definition of the function ι, defined in [11] and redefined further in this work (see Fig. 2). The function ι is equivalent to the carry bit that can occur throughout floating-point computations (generally $\iota = 1$). Intuitively, a too conservative static analysis would consider that a carry can be propagated at each operation, which corresponds to $\iota = 1$. This function becomes very costly if we perform several computations at a time and therefore the errors would be considerable. It is then crucial to use the most precise function ι. This is why, we reexamine in this work this function by sorting out the different cases where this function might be equal to 1 or 0: difference in magnitude of two floating-point numbers and the superposition of the *ulp* and the *ufp*, defined in Sect. 3.1, of these two numbers relative to each other. After that, the previous analysis will be expressed as a set of propositional formulas on linear constraints between integer variables only (checked by Z3). The transformed program is guaranteed to use variables of lower precision with a minimal number of bits than the original program. Second, we present the steps of construction of our new tool, POP, which executes and evaluates any kind of programs with respect to our grammar of a simple imperative language and including the implementation of the proposed approach. Also, we present some experimental results showing the efficiency of our mixed-precision tool in determining the minimal precision required.

The rest of this article is organized as follows. Section 2 introduces briefly some basic concepts related to the floating-point arithmetic and the related work of some existing precision tuning tools and we finish by introducing the overview of our approach. Section 3 deals with the forward and backward static error analysis by constraints generation with some examples. The implementation of our tool and the constraints resolution are presented in Sect. 4 and an experimental results are given in Sect. 5 before concluding in Sect. 6.

2   Overview

To better explain what POP does, a motivating example of a floating-point program is given in Fig. 1 which implements a simple scalar product of two vectors x and y presented with different magnitude of small and large floating-point values. For the vectors x and y, the variable values belong to $[1.0, 2.0]$, $[10.0, 15.0]$ and $[100.0, 110.0]$ for vector x and $[100.0, 110.0]$, $[5.0, 10.0]$ and $[450.0, 500.0]$ for vector y, respectively. In this example, we suppose that all variables are in double precision before analysis (original program in the left hand side of Fig. 1) and that a range determination is performed by dynamic analysis on these variables to make sure that no overflow can arise. We generate at each node of our program syntactic tree a unique control point in order to determine easily the final accuracy, after the forward and backward analysis, as shown on the left side of Fig. 1. It is conceivable that our program contains several annotations. First, for example on the left hand side of Fig. 1, the variables x_1 and y_1 are initialized to the abstract values $[1.0, 2.0]$ and $[10.0, 15.0]$ (in double precision) respectively, annotated with their control points thanks to the following annotations $x_1^{|1|} = [1.0, 2.0]^{|0|}$ and $y_1^{|3|} = [10.0, 15.0]^{|2|}$. As well, we have the statement

$$\texttt{require\_accuracy}(\texttt{v}, 23)^{|40|}$$

which informs the system that the user wants to turn on variable v to the simple precision at this control point. As a consequence, the minimal precision needed for the inputs and intermediary results satisfying the user assertion is observed on the right side of Fig. 1. For example, the variables x_1 passed from the double into float precision thanks to the annotation $x_1^{\#21} = [1.0, 2.0]^{\#22}$ (a floating-point number in single precision has 22 accurate digits). The results obtained show that POP, for present, automates precision tuning and propagates the user requirement along the program inputs and intermediary results.

3   Preliminary Notions

This section provides some background on the IEEE754 Standard of floating-point arithmetic, formats, rounding modes, errors and the *ufp* and *ulp* functions. Noting that several definitions of *ulp* exist in literature [12].

$$
\begin{aligned}
&x_1^{|1|} = [1.0, 2.0]^{|0|}; \\
&y_1^{|3|} = [10.0, 15.0]^{|2|}; \\
&z_1^{|5|} = [100.0, 110.0]^{|4|}; \\
&x_2^{|7|} = [100.0, 110.0]^{|6|}; \\
&y_2^{|9|} = [5.0, 10.0]^{|8|}; \\
&z_2^{|11|} = [450.0, 500.0]^{|10|}; \\
&v_1^{|17|} = x_1^{|13|} *^{|16|} x_2^{|15|}; \\
&v_2^{|23|} = y_1^{|19|} *^{|22|} y_2^{|21|}; \\
&v_3^{|29|} = z_1^{|25|} *^{|28|} z_2^{|27|}; \\
&v^{|38|} = v_1^{|31|} +^{|37|} v_2^{|33|} +^{|36|} v_3^{|35|}; \\
&\mathbf{require\_accuracy}(v, 23)^{|40|}
\end{aligned}
$$

$\xrightarrow{\substack{\text{POP}\\ Tool}}$

$$
\begin{aligned}
&x_1^{\#21} = [1.0, 2.0]^{\#22}; \\
&y_1^{\#14} = [10, 15]^{\#12}; \\
&z_1^{\#4} = [100.0, 110.0]^{\#3}; \\
&x_2^{\#21} = [100.0, 110.0]^{\#22}; \\
&y_2^{\#14} = [5.0, 10.0]^{\#12}; \\
&z_2^{\#4} = [450.0, 500.0]^{\#3}; \\
&v_1^{\#23} = x_1 *^{\#23} x_2; \\
&v_2^{\#15} = y_1 *^{\#14} y_2; \\
&v_3^{\#6} = z_1 *^{\#5} z_2; \\
&v^{\#23} = v_1 +^{\#23} v_2 +^{\#14} v_3; \\
&\mathbf{require\_accuracy}(v, 23)^{\#23}
\end{aligned}
$$

Fig. 1. Simple scalar product of two vectors program. The program on the left designs the initial program in double precision annotated with labels. On the right, the program after analysis annotated with the final accuracies at each label referring to the user requirement.

3.1 Basics on Floating-Point Arithmetic

The IEEE754 Standard formalizes a binary floating-point number x in base β (generally $\beta = 2$) as a triplet made of a sign, a mantissa and an exponent as shown in Eq. (1), where $s \in \{-1,1\}$ is the sign, m represents the mantissa, $m = d_0.d_1...d_{p-1}$, with the digits $0 \le d_i < \beta$, $0 \le i \le p - 1$, p is the precision (length of the mantissa) and the exponent $e \in [e_{min}, e_{max}]$.

$$x = s.m.\beta^{e-p+1} \tag{1}$$

Table 1. Parameters defining basic format floating-point numbers

Format	Name	Mantissa size (p - 1)	Size of e	e_{min}	e_{max}
Binary16	Half precision	10	5	-14	$+15$
Binary32	Single precision	23	8	-126	$+127$
Binary64	Double precision	52	11	-1122	$+1223$
Binary128	Quadruple precision	112	15	-16382	$+16383$

The IEEE754 Standard specifies some particular values for p, e_{min} and e_{max} [4]. Also, this standard defines binary formats (with $\beta = 2$) which are described in Table 1. Hence, the IEEE754 standard distinguishes between normalized and denormalized numbers. Indeed, the normalization of a floating-point number ensuring $d_0 \ne 0$ guarantees the uniqueness of its representation. Denormalized numbers make underflow gradual [13]. The IEEE754 standard defines also some special numbers. All these numbers are summarized in Table 2 (in Binary64).

Moreover, the IEEE754 Standard defines four rounding modes for elementary operations over floating-point numbers which are: towards $+\infty$, towards $-\infty$, towards zero and towards the nearest denoted by $\uparrow_{+\infty}$, $\uparrow_{-\infty}$, $\uparrow_0$ and $\uparrow_\sim$, respectively. Henceforth, we present the *ufp* (unit in the first place) and *ulp* (unit in the last place) functions which express the *weight of the most significant bit* and the *weight of the least significant bit*, respectively. In practice, these functions will be used further in this article to describe the error propagation across the computations. The definition of these functions is given in Eqs. (2) and (3) defined in [11].

$$ufp(x) = \min\{i \in \mathbb{Z} : 2^{i+1} > x\} = \lfloor \log_2(x) \rfloor \qquad (2)$$

Let p be the size of the significand, the *ulp* of a floating-point number can be expressed as shown:

$$ulp(x) = ufp(x) - p + 1. \qquad (3)$$

Table 2. Numbers in double precision

x	Exponent e	Mantissa m
$x = 0$ (if s = 0) $x = -0$ (if s = 1)	$e = 0$	$m = 0$
Normalized numbers $x = (-1)^s \times 2^{e-1023} \times 1.m$	$0 < e < 2047$	any
Denormalized numbers $x = (-1)^s \times 2^{e-1022} \times 0.m$	$e = 0$	$m \neq 0$
$x = +\infty$ (if s = 0) $x = -\infty$ (if s=0)	$e = 2047$	$m = 0$
$x = NaN$ (Not a Number)	$e = 2047$	$m \neq 0$

3.2   Related Work

There have been many efforts to automate the process of determining the best floating-point formats. Darulova and Kuncak [5] proposed a static analysis method to compute errors propagation. If their computed bound on the accuracy satisfies the post-conditions then the analysis is run again with a smaller format and it stops until finding the best format. Contrarily to our proposed tool, all their values have the same format (uniform-precision). Other methods rely on dynamic analysis. By way of illustration, Precimonious is considered as a dynamic automated search based tool that evaluates and executes different mixed-precision configurations of the program to identify the best configuration that satisfies the error threshold [15]. Also, we mention the Blame Analysis [16], a novel dynamic method that speeds up precision tuning by combining concrete and shadow program execution. The analysis determines the precision of all operands such that a given precision is achieved in the final result. So as to be more efficient with significant reduction in analysis time than used by itself,

Blame Analysis and Precimonious has been consolidated together and this combined approach has shown better results in term of program speedup compared to using Blame Analysis alone. Nonetheless, floating-point tuning of entire applications is not feasible yet, in this moment, by this method. Moreover, Lam et al. [10] instrument binary codes aiming to modify their precision without modifying the source codes. They also propose a dynamic search method to identify the parts of code where the precision should be modified. The major drawback of this tools is that the state space is exponential in the number of variables and exploring even a subset is very time-intensive.

Finally, there are various rigorous static analysis approaches that use interval and affine arithmetic or Taylor series approximations to analyze stability and to provide rigorous bounds on rounding errors. However, they do not scale very well and therefore have not been applied to high precision computing workloads. In this context, Chiang et al. [2] has proposed an approach which allocate a precision to the terms of only arithmetic expressions. Whereas they need to solve a quadratically constrained quadratic program to obtain their annotations. Also, Solovyev et al. [17] have proposed the FP-Taylor tool that implements a method to estimate round-off errors of floating-point computations called Symbolic Taylor Expansions.

4   Static Analysis by Constraints Generation

In this section, we refine the computations of the forward and backward transfer functions used by the POP tool for the cases of addition, product and subtraction done in [11]. These functions are defined using the *unit in the first* and *last places* introduced in Eqs. (2) and (3). Next, these functions will be formalized as a set of constraints made of propositional logic formulas and affine expressions among integers.

4.1   Forward and Backward Error Analysis

Forward Addition, Multiplication and Subtraction. Consequently, we introduce the forward transfer functions corresponding to the addition $\overrightarrow{\oplus}$, product $\overrightarrow{\otimes}$ and subtraction $\overrightarrow{\ominus}$ of two floating-point numbers $x \in \mathbb{F}_p$ and $y \in \mathbb{F}_q$ where $\mathbb{F}_p$ and $\mathbb{F}_q$ denote two sets of floating-point numbers in accuracy p and q, respectively. In Eq. (4), the operands $x_{p_{p'}}$ and $y_{q_{q'}}$ and their results $z_{r_{r'}}$ have respectively two parameters p, p', q, q' and r, r' which denote the correct precision of the result and of the error, respectively. Other than that, in distinction to [11], we introduce the truncation errors in order to be more precise through our computations. We denote the truncation errors by ε_+, $\varepsilon_\times$ and ε_- for the addition, product and subtraction operations respectively.

Definition 1. *The forward addition* $\overrightarrow{\oplus}$ *is given as shown in Eq. (4):*

$$\overrightarrow{\oplus}(x_{p_{p'}}, y_{q_{q'}}) = z_{r_{r'}} \quad where \quad r = ufp(x_{p_{p'}} + y_{q_{q'}}) - ufp(2^{ufp(x_{p_{p'}})-p+1} + 2^{ufp(y_{q_{q'}})-q+1} + 2^{ufp(z_{r_{r'}})-\sigma_+}) \tag{4}$$

In the sequel, we assume $x_{p_{p'}} = x$, $y_{q_{q'}} = y$ and $z_{r_{r'}} = z$. Let v be an exact value computed in infinite precision and the floating-point value is such that $\hat{v} = d_0.d_1...d_{p-1}.2^e$ of $\mathbb{F}_p$. The comparison of these two values is $|v - \hat{v}| \leq 2^{e-p+1}$. So, taking into account the definition of the function ufp in Eq. 2, we have for any $x \in \mathbb{F}_p$ and $y \in \mathbb{F}_q$ the error ε_x on x is bounded by:

$$\varepsilon_x < 2^{ulp(x)} = 2^{ufp(x)-p+1} \quad \text{and} \quad \varepsilon_y < 2^{ulp(y)} = 2^{ufp(y)-q+1} \tag{5}$$

The truncation error for the rounding mode towards the nearest $\uparrow_\sim$ defined by the IEEE754 Standard for the addition of x and y whose result is z is given by $\varepsilon_+ \leq 2^{\frac{1}{2}ulp(z)}$ and we have $ulp(z) = ufp(z) - \sigma_+ + 1$ where σ_+ presents the precision of the operator $+$. Thus, the truncation error is shown in Eq. 6:

$$\varepsilon_+ \leq 2^{ufp(z)-\sigma_+} \tag{6}$$

Definition 2. *The forward product $\vec{\otimes}$ is given as shown in Eq. (7):*

$$\vec{\otimes}(x_{p_{p'}}, y_{q_{q'}}) = z_{r_{r'}} \quad where \quad r = ufp(x_{p_{p'}} \times y_{q_{q'}}) - ufp(2^{ufp(x)+1}.2^{ufp(y)-q+1} + $$
$$2^{ufp(y)+1}.2^{ufp(x)-p+1} + 2^{ufp(x)-p+1}.2^{ufp(y)-q+1} + 2^{ufp(z)-\sigma_\times}) \tag{7}$$

We assume that the error $\varepsilon_{z_\times}$ of the multiplication of two floating-point numbers x and y whose result is z is $\varepsilon_{z_\times} = y \cdot \varepsilon_x + x \cdot \varepsilon_y + \varepsilon_x \cdot \varepsilon_y + \varepsilon_\times$ where $\varepsilon_\times$ is the truncation error for the product and is equal to $\varepsilon_\times \leq 2^{ufp(z)-\sigma_\times}$ (for the rounding mode towards $\uparrow_\sim$) and where $\sigma_\times$ represents the precision of the operator $\times$. So, the error $\varepsilon_{z_\times}$ could be bounded as shown in Eq. 8:

$$2^{ufp(x)} \leq x < 2^{ufp(x)+1} \quad \text{and} \quad 2^{ufp(y)} \leq y < 2^{ufp(y)+1}$$

and consequently,

$$\varepsilon_{z_\times} < 2^{ufp(x)+1}.2^{ufp(y)-q+1} + 2^{ufp(y)+1}.2^{ufp(x)-p+1} + 2^{ufp(x)-p+1}.2^{ufp(y)-q+1} + 2^{ufp(z)-\sigma_\times}$$

$$< 2^{ufp(x)+ufp(y)-q+2} + 2^{ufp(x)+ufp(y)-p+2} + 2^{ufp(x)+ufp(y)-p-q+2} + 2^{ufp(z)-\sigma_\times}$$

thus,

$$\varepsilon_{z_\times} \leq 2^{ufp(x)+ufp(y)-q+1} + 2^{ufp(x)+ufp(y)-p+1} + 2^{ufp(x)+ufp(y)-p-q+1} + 2^{ufp(z)-\sigma_\times}. \tag{8}$$

Definition 3. *The forward subtraction $\vec{\ominus}$ is given as shown in Eq. (9):*

$$\vec{\ominus}(x_{p_{p'}}, y_{q_{q'}}) = z_{r_{r'}} \quad where \quad r = ufp(x_{p_{p'}} - y_{q_{q'}}) - ufp(2^{ufp(x)-p+1} - 2^{ufp(y)-q+1} - $$
$$2^{ufp(z)-\sigma_-}) \tag{9}$$

Using the same approach in the addition case, we have $2^{ufp(x)} \leq x < 2^{ufp(x)+1}$ and $2^{ufp(y)} \leq y < 2^{ufp(y)+1}$ and the truncation error $\varepsilon_- \leq 2^{ufp(z)-\sigma_-}$ where σ_- is the precision of the operator -. The subtraction error between x and y is bounded as mentioned in Eq. (9).

Backward Addition, Subtraction and Multiplication. Equivalently, we introduce the backward transfer functions $\overleftarrow{\oplus}$, $\overleftarrow{\otimes}$ and $\overleftarrow{\ominus}$ which take advantage of the forward transfer functions and of the accuracy requirement on the results and by combining these two findings it is then possible to lower the number of bits needed for one of the operands. We consider that x is unknown where the result z and the operand y are known. The backward functions for the proposed arithmetic functions are given in the following properties.

Definition 4. *The backward transfer function for the addition $\overleftarrow{\oplus}$ is given as shown:*

$$\overleftarrow{\oplus}(z,y) = (z-y)_{p_{p'}} \quad with \quad p = ufp(z-y) - ufp(2^{ufp(z)-r+1} - 2^{ufp(y)-q+1} - 2^{ufp(x)-\sigma_+})$$
(10)

To apply the backward analysis, we assume that one of the operands is unknown (x in our case) while the result z is known. Then, we compute the precision p of the operand x with respect to the user accuracy requirement and the forward analysis result. As we said, the result and the operand errors can be bounded by $\varepsilon_{z_+} < 2^{ufp(z)-r+1}$ and $\varepsilon_y < 2^{ufp(y)-q+1}$ and for the truncation error is given as $\varepsilon_+ \leq 2^{ufp(x)-\sigma_+}$.

Definition 5. *We present the backward transfer function for the multiplication $\overleftarrow{\otimes}$ as shown:*

$$\overleftarrow{\otimes}(z,y) = (z \div y)_{p_{p'}} \quad with$$

$$p = ufp(z \div y) - ufp\left(\frac{2^{ufp(y)+1}.2^{ufp(z)-r+1} - 2^{ufp(z)+1}.2^{ufp(y)-q+1}}{2^{ufp(y)+1}(2^{ufp(y)+1} + 2^{ufp(y)-q+1}} - 2^{ufp(x)-\sigma_\times}\right)$$
(11)

In the case of product, we know that $\overleftarrow{\otimes}(z,y) = (z \div y)_{p_{p'}}$ with $p = ufp(z \div y) - ufp(\varepsilon_{z_\times})$ and where the truncation error $\varepsilon_\times \leq 2^{ufp(x)-\sigma_-}$ and the error $\varepsilon_{z_\times}$ is bounded as it is shown in Eq. (11).

Definition 6.

$$\overleftarrow{\ominus}(z,y) = (z+y)_{p_{p'}} \quad with \quad p = ufp(z+y) - ufp(2^{ufp(z)-r+1} + 2^{ufp(y)-q+1} + 2^{ufp(x)-\sigma_-})$$
(12)

We know that the roundoff errors are bounded as $\varepsilon_z < 2^{ufp(z)-r+1}$ and $\varepsilon_y < 2^{ufp(y)-q+1}$ and the truncation error $\varepsilon_- \leq 2^{ufp(x)-\sigma_-}$ where σ_- denotes the precision of the operator - and the error in Eq. (12) is given as $\varepsilon_{z_-} = \varepsilon_x - \varepsilon_y - \varepsilon_-$.

Obviously, our static analysis does not work on scalar values as in Eqs. (4) to (12) but on intervals instead. As described in [11], we abstract sets of values of $\mathbb{F}_p$

using the following connection in Eq. (13) where an element $i^{\sharp} \in \mathbb{I}_p$ correspond to $i^{\sharp} = [\underline{f}, \overline{f}]_p$ is defined by two floating-point numbers and an accuracy p.

$$\mathbb{I}_p \ni [\underline{f}, \overline{f}]_p = \{f \in \mathbb{F}_p : \underline{f} \leq f \leq \overline{f}\} \quad with \quad \mathbb{I} = \bigcup_{p \in \mathbb{N}} \mathbb{I}_p. \tag{13}$$

The operations $\overrightarrow{\oplus}^{\sharp}$, $\overleftarrow{\oplus}^{\sharp}$, $\overrightarrow{\otimes}^{\sharp}$ and $\overleftarrow{\otimes}^{\sharp}$ among values of $\mathbb{I}_p$ are defined in [11] in function of $\overrightarrow{\oplus}$, $\overleftarrow{\oplus}$, $\overrightarrow{\otimes}$ and $\overleftarrow{\otimes}$. For the rest of the article, we deal with the generation of constraints only for the addition and the product.

4.2   Constraints Generation

In this section, we describe how to generate constraints to determine the lowest precision on variables and intermediary values in programs. An important definition of the function ι, computed on floating-point numbers, is given in this section. By this definition, we attempt to be far more efficient in the way we propagate errors across the arithmetic operations. The methodical difference between the function $\iota(u, v)$ proposed in [11] and our new definition $\iota(t, u, v, w)$ is that we take in consideration the ufp and ulp of the two operands in order to compare the two floating-point number errors α and β and we add an extra bit only if we are certain that $ulp(\alpha)$ is lesser than the $ufp(\beta)$ (0 otherwise). Compared to the former definition of [11], our new definition improves significantly the accuracy of the static analysis by being less pessimistic. As mentioned earlier, the transfer functions previously seen in Sect. 4.1 are not translated directly into constraints because the resulting system would be too difficult to solve and contain non-linear constraints. Therefore, we reduce the problem to a constraint system consisting in propositional formulas on linear relations between integer elements only. In what follows, we introduce the constraints that we generate for the arithmetic expressions in which we are interested.

Forward Operations. Back to Eqs. (4) to (12), our goal is to compute the correct precision r and the precision r' of the result error (ε_{z_+} for the addition and $\varepsilon_{z_\times}$ for the product) for the floating-point number z. Intuitively, we compute $z = x + y$ with related errors ε_x and ε_y and ε_{z_+} and we want to compute $ufp(\varepsilon_{z_+})$ in function of the errors on the operands.

Proposition 1. *Let x in $\mathbb{F}_p$ and y in $\mathbb{F}_q$ and let z the result of the addition operation between these two floating-point numbers. We have in the worst case a carry bit that can occur through this operation as it has been proven in [12].*

$$ufp(z) \leq max(ufp(x), ufp(y)) + 1 \tag{14}$$

As a matter of fact, the previous Eq. (14) is considered as correct but pessimistic (too large over-approximation) due to the fact that adding an extra bit specially for cases we would not to, becomes very costly if we perform several computations. In previous work [11], a new function ι was presented in order to refine Eq. (14): they compare the unit in the first places of the operands and they add an extra bit only if they are equal which is correct but it misses exactness. In this work, we present our new definition of function ι. In fact, let x in $\mathbb{F}_p$ and y in $\mathbb{F}_q$, our strategy is to compare $ulp(x)$ with $ufp(y)$ and conversely ($ulp(y)$ with $ufp(x)$). In Definition 7, we present function ι and in Fig. 2 we present an example of cases of function ι where an extra bit can occur ($\iota = 1$) or not ($\iota = 0$).

Definition 7. *We introduce the function $\iota(t, u, v, w)$ as the exceeding of 1 bit that can occur in operations between the floating-point numbers.*

$$\iota(t, u, v, w) = \begin{cases} 0 & u > t \ or \ w > u, \\ 1 & otherwise. \end{cases} \tag{15}$$

Proposition 2. *In order to compute the function ι, we need to compute the unit in the last places $ulp(\alpha)$ and $ulp(\beta)$. Considering p' the precision of α, from Eq. (3) we have $ulp(\alpha) = ufp(\alpha) - p' + 1$ where $ufp(\alpha) = ufp(x) - p$. Consequently, we obtain that:*

$$ulp(\alpha) = ufp(x) - p - p' + 1 \tag{16}$$

We know from Eq. (3) that for $x \in \mathbb{F}_p$ the unit in the last place is $ulp(x) = ufp(x) - p + 1$. This definition is also valid for $ulp(\varepsilon_x)$ with p' the precision of ε_x and also we deduce that if $ulp(x) = ufp(x) - p + 1$ than $ufp(\varepsilon_x) = ufp(x) - p$ and than we obtain the result in Eq. (16).

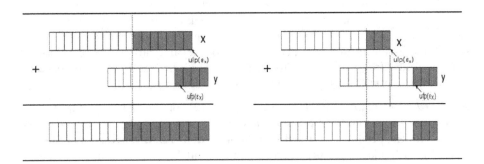

Fig. 2. Definition of function ι. The figure on the left represents the case of $\iota(\alpha, \beta) = 1$ and so an exceeding bit can occur throughout computations. The figure on the right is equivalent to $\iota(\alpha, \beta) = 0$

Forward Addition: From Definition 7, Eq. (5) and Eq. (14), we present Proposition (3). As we said before, if we sum $z = x + y$ the error is equal to $\varepsilon_{z_+} = \varepsilon_x + \varepsilon_y + \varepsilon_+$. Now, in order to apply the definition of the function ι, we will disassociate the total error ε_{z_+} into two errors: the roundoff error $\varepsilon_{xy} = \varepsilon_x + \varepsilon_y$ and the truncation error ε_+. Also, we will manage by presenting one case of the ι function ($u > t$).

Proposition 3. *Let* $a = ufp(x)$, $b = ufp(y)$ *and* $c = ufp(z)$,

$$ufp(\varepsilon_{xy}) < \max(a - p + 1, b - q + 1) + \iota(a - p - p' + 1, b - q) \qquad (17)$$

Taking into account Eq. (17) above, $ufp(\varepsilon_{z_+})$ is then bounded by:

$$ufp(\varepsilon_{z_+}) < \max\left(\max\left((a-p+1, b-q+1) + \iota(a-p-p'+1, b-q), c-\sigma_+\right)\right) + \iota(a-p-p'+1, b-q) \quad (18)$$

which implies that the precision of the result z in this addition is

$$r = ufp(x+y) - \max\left(\max\left((a-p+1, b-q+1) + \iota(a-p, b-q), c-\sigma_+\right)\right) - \iota(a-p-p'+1, b-q). \quad (19)$$

Proof. Formally, let $\alpha = \sum\limits_{i=n_0}^{n_1} \alpha_i 2^i$ and $\beta = \sum\limits_{i=m_0}^{m_1} \beta_i 2^i$ two floating-point numbers. Let us assume that $n_1 < m_0$. From Definition 7, we have $ufp(\alpha) = n_1$ and $ulp(\beta) = n_0$ then:

$$\alpha + \beta = \sum_{i=n_1}^{m_0} \gamma_i 2^i \quad \text{where} \quad \gamma_i = \begin{cases} \alpha_i & \text{if } i \in [n_0, n_1], \\ \beta_i & \text{if } i \in [m_0, m_1] \\ 0 & \text{otherwise.} \end{cases}$$

Finally, we conclude that $ufp(\varepsilon_{z_+}) = m_1$. In the case where $n_0 > m_1$, we deduce that $ufp(\varepsilon_{z_+}) = n_1$. After, from Eq. (18), we substitute the new refinement over-approximation of the total error ε_{z_+} and consequently we deduce the precision r in Eq. (19).

Now, what remains to be done is to determine the precision of the error r' of the addition. That's why, we need to compute $ulp(\epsilon_{z_+})$ as it is shown in Eq. (20). In the case of addition, we present $ulp(\varepsilon_{z_+})$ as the smallest ulp between the two operands errors ($ulp(\varepsilon_x)$ and $ulp(\varepsilon_y)$) and we conclude finally that the precision of the error $r' = ufp(\epsilon_{z_+}) - ulp(\epsilon_{z_+})$.

$$ulp(\varepsilon_{z_+}) = min\left(ulp(\varepsilon_x), ulp(\varepsilon_y)\right) \qquad (20)$$

Forward Multiplication. For the multiplication case, we apply our new Definition 7 and Eq. (8) and we present Proposition 4.

Proposition 4. *Let a and b and c three integers with $a = ufp(x)$, $b = ufp(y)$ and $c = ufp(z)$. We apply the same proceeding as in the forward addition, we dissociate the total error $\varepsilon_\times$ into the roundoff error $\varepsilon_{xy} = \varepsilon_x + \varepsilon_y$ and the truncation error $\varepsilon_\times$. So, we have:*

$$ufp(\varepsilon_{xy}) < \max(a + b - p + 1, a + b - q + 1) + \iota(a - p - p' + 1, b - q) \qquad (21)$$

and then the total error $ufp(\varepsilon_{z\times})$ is given as

$$ufp(\varepsilon_{z\times}) < \max\left(\max\left((a - p + 1, b - q + 1) + \iota(a - p - p' + 1, b - q), c - \sigma_+\right)\right) + \iota(a - p - p' + 1, b - q) \quad (22)$$

and then we deduce that

$$r = ufp(x \times y) - \max\left(\max\left((a-p+1, b-q+1) + \iota(a-p, b-q), c-\sigma_+\right)\right) - \iota(a-p-p'+1, b-q).$$
(23)

Next, like we have proceed in Eq. (20) in the case of addition we may say that the unit in the last place of $\varepsilon_{z_\times}$ is defined by

$$ulp(\varepsilon_{z_\times}) = ulp(\epsilon_x) + ulp(\epsilon_y)$$
(24)

By reasoning in the same way, we linearize the computations for the backward operations (addition and multiplication).

Backward Addition: We consider now the backward transfer functions, depending on Eq. (10) for the addition case. We know that $p = ufp(z - y) - ufp(\varepsilon_z - \varepsilon_y - \varepsilon_+)$. So, again let $c = ufp(z)$ we can over-approximate ε_z thanks to the relations $\varepsilon_z < 2^{c-r+1}$, $\varepsilon_y \geq 0$ and $\varepsilon_+ \geq 0$ and consequently

$$p = ufp(z - y) - c + r.$$
(25)

Backward Multiplication: Again, we take $a = ufp(x)$, $b = ufp(y)$ and $c = ufp(z)$. From Eq. (11), we know that $2^c \leq z < 2^{c+1}$, $2^b \leq y < 2^{b+1}$ and $\varepsilon_{z_\times} < 2^{c-r+1}$, $\varepsilon_y < 2^{b-q+1}$ which implies that $y.\varepsilon_{z_\times} - z.\varepsilon_y < 2^{c+b-r+2} - 2^{b+c-q+2}$ and that

$$\frac{1}{y.(y + \varepsilon_y)} < 2^{-2b}.$$

Consequently,

$$\varepsilon_{z_\times} \leq 2^{-2b}.(2^{c+b-r+2} - 2^{b+c-q+2}) - 2^{a-\sigma_\times} \leq 2^{c-b-r+1} - 2^{c-b-q+1} - 2^{a-\sigma_\times}$$

and finally,

$$p = ufp(z \div y) - \max(\max(c - b - r + 1, c - b - q + 1), a - \sigma_\times).$$
(26)

5   The POP Tool

In this section, we present our tool, POP: Precision OPtimizer. We present its architecture, its input including the program file annotated with the developer accuracy expectation, parameters and its outputs. Also, we illustrate the mechanism followed by POP to lower the precision of the floating-point programs.

5.1   Architecture

At this stage, we present the main architecture of POP also described in Fig. 3. POP is written in JAVA while each expression, boolean and statement presented in Fig. 4 are represented as packages gathering the different classes of their definition. We can illustrate the tool hierarchy as follows:

- **Parser:** It takes a file of a floating-point program referring to our simple imperative language. Before evaluating our program, we call the ANTLR: (ANother Tool for Language Recognition) [14] framework in order to generate, from a grammar file, a parser that can build and walk parse tree.
- **Range determination:** Consists in launching the execution of the program a certain number of times in order to determine dynamically the range of variables (we plan to use a static analyzer in the future).
- **Constraints generation:** It implements the forward and backward error analysis transfer function seen in Sect. 4 where the main semantics are detailed in [11]. In addition to the variables of accuracy assigned to each label ℓ which are $acc_F(\ell)$, $acc_B(\ell)$ and $acc(\ell)$ (defined in Sect. 5.2), we add new constraints relative to the *ulp* and the precision of the error in order to compute correctly the function ι discussed in Sect. 4.2.
- **Constraints resolution:** Firstly, we call the Z3 SMT solver [6] to find a solution for our constraints and we implement a cost function (see Sect. 6) to refine the solutions obtained in term of optimality. In future work, we will explore a new resolution method based on policy iterations [8]. Concerning the complexity of the analysis performed by POP, in practice, the analysis is carried out by the SMT solver which solves the constraints. The number of variables and constraints is linear in the size of the program. The complexity to analyze a program of size n is then equivalent to that of solving a system of n constraints in our language of constraints (by the solver).

5.2   Simple Imperative Language of Constraints

In order to explain the constraints generation, we introduce the following simple imperative language. As it is mentioned in Fig. 4, we assign to each element of our language (expression, boolean and statement) a unique label $\ell \in lab$ with the intention of identifying without ambiguity each node of the syntactic tree. The same strategy as in [11] is adopted, the statement require_accuracy$(x, n)^\ell$ denotes the accuracy that x must have at the control point ℓ. Therefore, we assign to each control point ℓ three integer variables corresponding to the forward, the backward and the final accuracies so that the inequality in Eq. (27) is verified. Hence, we notice that in the forward mode, the accuracy decreases contrarily to the backward mode when we strengthen the post-conditions (accuracy increases).

$$0 \leq acc_B(\ell) \leq acc(\ell) \leq acc_F(\ell) \tag{27}$$

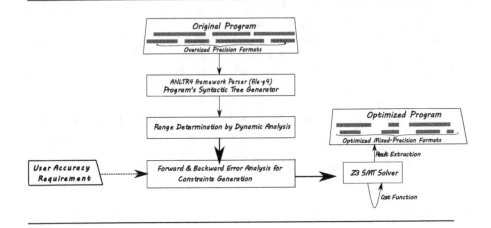

Fig. 3. POP mixed-precision analysis architecture

Expression : e ::= $c\sharp p^\ell$ | id^ℓ | $e_1^{\ell_1} +^\ell e_2^{\ell_2}$ | $e_1^{\ell_1} -^\ell e_2^{\ell_2}$ | $e_1^{\ell_1} \times^\ell e_2^{\ell_2}$ | $e_1^{\ell_1} \div^\ell e_2^{\ell_2}$
Boolean : b ::= true | false | $e_1^{\ell_1} <^\ell e_2^{\ell_2}$ | $e_1^{\ell_1} >^\ell e_2^{\ell_2}$ | $e_1^{\ell_1} =^\ell e_2^{\ell_2}$
Statement : c ::= $c_1^{\ell_1}; c_2^{\ell_2}$ | $id =^\ell e^{\ell_1}$ | **while**$^\ell$ b^{ℓ_0} **do** $c_1^{\ell_1}$ | **if**$^\ell$ b^{ℓ_0} **then** $c_1^{\ell_1}$ **else** c |
require_accuracy(x,n)$^\ell$

Fig. 4. Simple imperative language of constraints

6   Experimental Results

In this section, we aim at evaluating the performance of POP which generates the constraints defined in Sect. 4.2 and calls the Z3 SMT solver in order to obtain a solution. The solutions returned by Z3 are not unique due to the fact that it is not an optimizer but a solver. To surpass this limitation, we add to our global system of constraints an additional constraint related to a cost function ϕ (we take the same definition in [11]). The purpose of a cost function $\phi(c)$ of a given program c is to compute the sum of the accuracies of all the variables and the intermediary values collected in each label of the arithmetic expressions as it is shown in Eq. (28).

$$\phi(c) = \sum_{x \in Id, \ell \in Lab} acc(x^\ell) + \sum_{\ell \in Lab} acc(\ell) \qquad (28)$$

After, our tool searches the smallest integer P such that our system of constraints admits a solution. Consequently, we start the binary search with $P \in [0, 52 \times n]$ where all the values are in double precision and where n is the number of terms in Eq. (28). While a solution is found for a given value of P, a new iteration of the binary search is run with a smaller value of P. When the solver fails for some P, a new iteration of the binary search is run with a larger P and we continue this process until convergence. We ran our precision-tuning analysis on programs that perform sum and product operations only (for now) to show the performances of our forward and backward analysis described in Sect. 4.2. Noting that these operations are widely used in embedded systems, graphic processing, finance, etc. We take into consideration two examples which consist in a rotation matrix-vector multiplication and the computation of the determinant of 3×3 matrices and we present in Fig. 5 some measures of the efficiency of our analysis on these two examples. We assume that in the original programs of our examples all the variables are in double precision.

Rotation Matrix-Vector Multiplication

Our first example consists in a rotation matrix R which is used in the rotation of vectors and tensors while the coordinate system remains fixed. For instance, we want to rotate a vector around the z axis by angle θ. The rotation matrix and the rotated column vectors are given by:

$$\begin{bmatrix} cos\theta & -sin\theta & 0 \\ sin\theta & cos\theta & 0 \\ 0 & 0 & 1 \end{bmatrix} \begin{bmatrix} x \\ y \\ z \end{bmatrix} = \begin{bmatrix} x' \\ y' \\ z' \end{bmatrix}$$

We aim from this experimentation to compute the performance of our POP tool from different angles of rotation $\frac{\pi}{3}$, $\frac{\pi}{4}$ and $\frac{\pi}{6}$, a variety of input vectors chosen with difference in magnitude $A = [1.0, 2.0, 3.0]$, $B = [10.0, 100.0, 500.0]$, $C = [100.0, 500.0, 1000.0]$, $D = [-100.0, -10.0, 1000.0]$, $E = [1.0, 2.0, 500.0]$ and $F = [1.0, 500.0, 10000.0]$ and for different user accuracy requirements 10, 15, 20, 25, 30 and 35. This example generates 858 constraints and 642 variables which are very manageable by the Z3 solver. Initially starting with 10335 bits for the original program (only variables in double precision), Fig. 5c shows that the improvement, in the number of bits needed to realize the user requirements, compared to the initial number of bits, ranges from 38 % to 87 % which confirms the usefulness of our analysis. Also, we can observe in Fig. 5e that the majority of variables fits in single precision format for an accuracy ≤ 35 and that no double precision variables are noticed for vectors A, B, C, D and E for an accuracy 15. For this example, we found that the variation of the angles of rotation do not have impact on the number of double precision variables after analysis that's why we choose only the angle $\frac{\pi}{4}$ in Fig. 5e and by modifying the magnitude of the vectors at every turn. Besides, POP assigns zeros to the accuracies of the variables that are not used by the program.

Determinant of 3 × 3 Matrices

Our second example computes the determinant $det(M)$ of a 3×3 matrices $M1$, $M2$ and $M3$ as shown:

$$M = \begin{bmatrix} a & b & c \\ d & e & f \\ g & h & i \end{bmatrix} \rightarrow det(M) = (a.e.i + d.h.c + g.b.f) - (g.e.c + a.h.f + d.b.i)$$

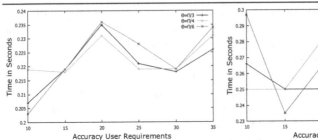

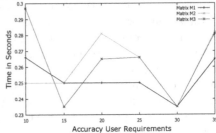

(a) Precision tuning tool execution time for the rotation matrix-vector multiplication

(b) Precision tuning tool execution time for the a 3×3 matrix determinant

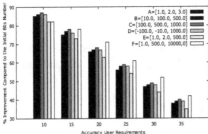

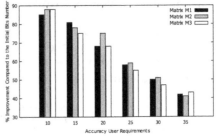

(c) Optimization of the number of bits compared to the original rotation matrix-vector multiplication program

(d) Optimization of the number of bits compared to the original 3×3 determinant program

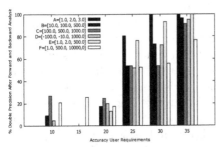

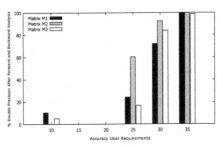

(e) The percentage of the double precision variables after the forward and backward analysis for the first example for $\theta = \frac{\pi}{4}$

(f) The percentage of the double precision variables after the forward and backward analysis for the second example

Fig. 5. Measures of the efficiency of the analysis on the two input examples: the time execution measure, the optimization of the number of bits of the transformed programs compared to the original ones and the percentage of the double precision variables after analysis.

The matrices coefficients belong to multiple magnitude ranges: $M1 =$
$$\begin{bmatrix} [-50.1,50.1] & [-50.1,50.1] & [-50.1,50.1] \\ [-10.1,10.1] & [-10.1,10.1] & [-10.1,10.1] \\ [-5.1,5.1] & [-5.1,5.1] & [-5.1,5.1] \end{bmatrix}, M2 = \begin{bmatrix} [-100.1,100.1] & [-100.1,100.1] & [-100.1,100.1] \\ [-10.1,10.1] & [-10.1,10.1] & [-10.1,10.1] \\ [-2.1,2.1] & [-2.1,2.1] & [-2.1,2.1] \end{bmatrix}$$ and

$$M3 = \begin{bmatrix} [-10.1,10.1] & [-10.1,10.1] & [-10.1,10.1] \\ [-20.1,20.1] & [-20.1,20.1] & [-20.1,20.1] \\ [-5.1,5.1] & [-5.1,5.1] & [-5.1,5.1] \end{bmatrix}.$$ With 686 number of variables and 993 generated constraints, POP finds the minimal precision of the inputs and intermediary results for this example in less than 0.3 s as it is observed in Fig. 5b (time only for the resolution of the system of constraints and the calls of the Z3 SMT solver done by binary search) for different requirements of accuracy. Hence, as viewed in our first example, the final number of bits of the transformed program compared to 9964 initial bits is considerable as shown in Fig. 5d. Finally, we notice that our analysis succeeded in turning off almost the double precision variables to a fairly rounded single precision ones for an accuracy ≤ 20.

7 Conclusions and Future Work

In this article, we have introduced POP, an automated tuning tool for floating-point precision that computes the minimal number of bits needed for the variables and intermediary results in order to accomplish the user requirement of accuracy. Also, we have explained in details our forward and backward static analysis, done by abstract interpretation. Moreover, we have shown that we can express our analysis as a set of constraints made of propositional logic formulas and relations between affine expressions over integers which can be easily checked by an SMT solver. Obviously, our approach can be extended to other language structures in particular arrays and functions. Besides, we have considered that a range determination is performed by dynamic analysis on the variables of our programs and that no overflow arises during our analysis but from this time on we would like to adopt a static analyzer in order to infer safe ranges on our variables.

In future work, we would like to explore the policy iteration method [8] as a replacement for the non-optimizing solver (Z3) coupled to a binary search used in this article. In fact, we aim to apply the policy iteration method to improve the accuracy. The principle consists in transforming all the generated constraints to the form of min-max of discrete affine maps. Further, it will be interesting to feed the policy iteration with the Z3 solution as an initial policy and consequently comparing the solutions of these two methods in term of execution time and optimality. Nevertheless, our goal is to validate experimentally our tool on codes from various fields including safety-critical systems such as control systems for vehicles, medical equipment and industrial plants. Also, we are currently working on exploring the precision tuning in a new unexplored domain, Internet of Things. In fact, the type of problems of energy consumption and memory saving are widespread in this area that is why we are working on tuning the precision of the basic buildings of common IoT items such as accelerometers and gyroscopes. Conclusively, comparing our tool to other existing tools in the matter of analysis time and speed and the quality of the solution is a tremendous challenge to examine.

References

1. Patriot missile defense: Software problem led to system failure at Dhahran, Saudi Arabia. Technical report GAO/IMTEC-92-26, General Accounting Office (1992)
2. Chiang, W.F., Baranowski, M., Briggs, I., Solovyev, A., Gopalakrishnan, G., Rakamarić, Z.: Rigorous floating-point mixed-precision tuning. In: Proceedings of the 44th ACM SIGPLAN Symposium on Principles of Programming Languages (POPL). ACM (2017)
3. Cousot, P., Cousot, R.: Abstract interpretation: a unified lattice model for static analysis of programs by construction or approximation of fixpoints. In: Conference Record of the Fourth ACM Symposium on Principles of Programming Languages, Los Angeles, California, USA, January 1977, pp. 238–252 (1977)
4. Damouche, N., Martel, M.: Salsa: an automatic tool to improve the numerical accuracy of programs. In: Shankar, N., Dutertre, B. (eds.) Automated Formal Methods. Kalpa Publications in Computing, EasyChair (2018)
5. Darulova, E., Kuncak, V.: Sound compilation of reals. In: Proceedings of the 41st ACM SIGPLAN-SIGACT Symposium on Principles of Programming Languages, POPL 2014. ACM (2014)
6. de Moura, L., Bjørner, N.: Z3: an efficient SMT solver. In: Ramakrishnan, C.R., Rehof, J. (eds.) TACAS 2008. LNCS, vol. 4963, pp. 337–340. Springer, Heidelberg (2008). https://doi.org/10.1007/978-3-540-78800-3_24
7. De Moura, L., Bjørner, N.: Satisfiability modulo theories: introduction and applications. Commun. ACM **54**(9), 69–77 (2011)
8. Gaubert, S., Goubault, E., Taly, A., Zennou, S.: Static analysis by policy iteration on relational domains. In: De Nicola, R. (ed.) Programming Languages and Systems. Springer, Heidelberg (2007)
9. Halfhill, T.R.: The truth behind the Pentium bug: how often do the five empty cells in the Pentium's FPU lookup table spell miscalculation? (1995)
10. Lam, M.O., Hollingsworth, J.K., de Supinski, B.R., Legendre, M.P.: Automatically adapting programs for mixed-precision floating-point computation. In: Proceedings of the 27th International ACM Conference on International Conference on Supercomputing, ICS 2013. ACM (2013)
11. Martel, M.: Floating-point format inference in mixed-precision. In: Barrett, C., Davies, M., Kahsai, T. (eds.) NFM 2017. LNCS, vol. 10227, pp. 230–246. Springer, Cham (2017). https://doi.org/10.1007/978-3-319-57288-8_16
12. Muller, J.M.: On the definition of ULP(x). Research Report RR-5504, LIP RR-2005-09, INRIA, LIP, February 2005. https://hal.inria.fr/inria-00070503
13. Muller, J.M., et al.: Handbook of Floating-Point Arithmetic, 1st edn. Birkhäuser, Boston (2009)
14. Parr, T.: The Definitive ANTLR 4 Reference, 2nd edn. Pragmatic Bookshelf, Raleigh (2013)
15. Rubio-González, C., et al.: Precimonious: tuning assistant for floating-point precision. In: International Conference for High Performance Computing, Networking, Storage and Analysis, SC 2013, Denver, CO, USA, 17–21 November 2013 (2013)
16. Rubio-González, C., et al.: Floating-point precision tuning using blame analysis. In: 2016 IEEE/ACM 38th International Conference on Software Engineering (ICSE) (2016)
17. Solovyev, A., Jacobsen, C., Rakamarić, Z., Gopalakrishnan, G.: Rigorous estimation of floating-point round-off errors with symbolic Taylor expansions. In: Bjørner, N., de Boer, F. (eds.) FM 2015. LNCS, vol. 9109, pp. 532–550. Springer, Cham (2015). https://doi.org/10.1007/978-3-319-19249-9_33

Visualising Railway Safety Verification

Filippos Pantekis[ID], Phillip James[(⊠)][ID], Liam O'Reilly[ID],
Daniel Archambault[ID], and Faron Moller[ID]

Department of Computer Science, Swansea University, Swansea, Wales, UK
{filippos.pantekis,p.d.james,l.p.oreilly,d.w.archambault,
f.g.moller}@swansea.ac.uk

Abstract. The application of formal methods to the railway domain has a long-standing history within the academic community. Many approaches can provide both successful proofs of safety and, in the case of failure, traces explaining the failure. However, if a given model does produce a failure, it is difficult to understand the conditions that led to the issue. We present a method to visualise railway safety issues to help engineers and researchers explore the problem so that they can adjust their designs accordingly. We evaluate our approach through qualitative real-world case studies with researchers and railway engineers.

1 Introduction

Railway signalling represents an example of safety critical control systems. As such, the use of rigorous development processes using formal methods has been extensively studied by the academic community [1,6,11,13–16,19,20,24,27]. Such approaches involve automatically producing a mathematical proof that the control system under consideration obeys certain rules regarding safety. However, uptake of such methods by industry has been hindered by the challenges of: *scalability* (the proposed mathematical proof techniques do not scale to large industrial examples); *faithfulness* (the models created fail to capture the intricacies of modern railway signalling, which are often supplier dependent); and *usability* (existing tools for formal analysis are not necessarily accessible to signalling engineers). In recent years, the formal methods community has proposed solutions to scalability [25] and faithfulness [21]. However accessibility remains an open challenge.

In this paper, we present a visualisation system for understanding safety issues in scheme plans, specifically (1) a method to draw scheme plans that is useful for railway engineers, supporting interoperability between toolsets; and (2) a dynamic visualisation technique to view key frames pertaining to safety issues in context. We evaluate these approaches with railway engineers from Siemens Rail UK and academics working in formal methods. The feedback provides evidence that our algorithm for track layout is a useful way to improve tool interoperability, whilst the evaluation of our visualisation approach for counterexamples suggests that experienced users can quickly identify issues with designs.

© Springer Nature Switzerland AG 2020
O. Hasan and F. Mallet (Eds.): FTSCS 2019, CCIS 1165, pp. 95–105, 2020.
https://doi.org/10.1007/978-3-030-46902-3_6

2   Related Work

In this section, we give a brief review of the field of formal methods and its application to railways, before considering approaches to railway graph layout and how they relate to our approach.

2.1   Railway Verification

Formal verification aims to provide a rigorous mathematical argument to show that a system or design meets a given requirement. A typical application area for formal methods is safety critical systems, of which railway control systems are a clear example. Many approaches apply formal methods to railway safety verification [1,6,11–16,19,20,24,27], with much of this work focusing on the scientific development and application of results to examples in industry. However, uptake of these results by industry is impeded by complex notations and the heavy mathematical constructions that are involved [21].

Recently, there have been advances focusing on the accessibility of these approaches. Specifically, toolsets that support domain specific languages [17, 21] and graphical specification development environments [18,22] have allowed railway engineers to model and verify systems in notations that are natural. However, when a verification attempt fails, methods for presenting the reasons for failure are lacking.

Another limitation with existing toolsets is that users are often required to re-draw and re-enter railway layouts directly into the verification toolset when geospatial information for track plans is unavailable. Re-entering data is clearly cumbersome and time consuming, whilst importation of verification data tends to be hard as geospatial information is often missing from the data.

In this paper, we address these points by adapting visualisation research results to this area. In particular, we apply energy-based graph layout approaches to automatically import and derive geospatial information for track plans. We then utilize approaches to key frame visualisation in order to provide feedback on failed verification attempts. We have incorporated these into the OnTrack railway verification toolset [22] and have evaluated the work with end users.

2.2   Graph Layout for Railways

Railway track plans illustrate how various railway lines are connected at stations and junctions, and can be interpreted (and drawn) as graphs. Such depictions are natural for engineers working within the railway domain and can be of benefit in visualising points of failure. However, they are less relevant with respect to the correct functioning of the railway.

Existing approaches to drawing metro maps and network layouts [7,26,30,31] provide possible methods for visualising track plans. Here, stations are placed in the plane, with their spread-out geographic locations taken into account alongside desirable æsthetic properties. For track plans, however, we deal with small geospatial areas with complex network topologies; geospatial considerations are far less important to us, and in any case are typically unavailable (particularly if the railway system has not been built).

In order to draw the track plan automatically, we use energy-based methods for graph drawing [4, 8, 23]. These methods modify the graph locally using a scoring function to determine if the layout has improved based on the selected æsthetic criteria. Such methods have been used for general graph drawing but have not been adapted for track layout. We create a method that optimises for the desired properties of track plans, making drawings useful for domain scientists and railway engineers.

2.3 Dynamic Data Visualisation

Visualising a railway safety issue – such as how two trains might collide – requires a visualisation of the track plan and the trains that are moving on it. This is a dynamic multivariate graph visualisation problem [5] where the attributes (trains and point/signal states) are dynamic but the network topology remains the same.

There has been significant work in the area of dynamic data visualisation. In much of this work, animation is of benefit if it is a short animated transition around a key event [2, 29]. Experimental results [3] have found that a "small multiples" representation (visualising dynamic attributes as colour on a static graph) can provide lower user response times with no significant difference in error when compared to animation.

In the railway verification community, signalling engineers often step through safety failures like mathematicians step through the lines of a proof. Our visualisation must not only be perceptually effective, it must also support the cognitive map with which railway engineers and formal methods researchers approach the problem. We thus provide an interactive step-through approach, with support for small multiples around key events.

3 Railway Visualisation Methods

In this section, we present our simulated annealing algorithm [8] for computing a railway layout, followed by details concerning our counterexample visualisation using key frames.

For our purposes, railway track plans are comprised of: track segments (TS); and points, which may be left-facing (LFP) or right-facing (RFP), and whose straight and offshoot tracks are designated as normal (N) or reverse (R), one of each. (The specific purposes of these distinctions is unimportant for this paper.)

A *railway graph* $RG = (V, E)$ is an undirected graph where the vertices are either track segments or points: $V = TS \cup LFP \cup RFP$. A track plan layout is an assignment of two-dimensional positions (x, y) for all vertices in the railway graph.

3.1   The Simulated Annealing Layout Algorithm

To establish a good layout for a track plan (i.e., such that it conforms with validity criteria and is therefore understood by railway engineers), we employ a simulated annealing algorithm [8]. This algorithm is given as follows:

> $\ell \leftarrow$ initial (random) layout;
> temp $\leftarrow$ nodeCount(ℓ); $- -$ *initial temperature*
> best $\leftarrow \ell$;
> iter $\leftarrow 0$;
> <u>while</u> temp > 0 <u>do</u>:
>   iter $\leftarrow$ iter+1;
> $\ell \leftarrow$ tweak(ℓ, temp);
>   <u>if</u> $\nu(\ell) > \nu(best)$ <u>or</u> rand$(0,1) < \exp\left(\frac{\nu(\ell) - \nu(best)}{temp}\right)$
>   <u>then</u> best $\leftarrow \ell$;
>   <u>if</u> iter mod $\lfloor$temp$*$c$\rfloor = 0$
>   <u>then</u> temp $\leftarrow \lfloor$temp$*$d$\rfloor$
>   <u>return</u> best

Each point is initialised with a random type from the sets LFP and RFP (as determined by the given data) to provide an initial layout. This layout is then repeatedly tweaked in an effort to discover an optimal (best) layout.

There are three essential components to our algorithm: a *temperature (temp)*; a *valuation* function ν for rating layouts; and the *tweak* function.

- From an initial value (equal to the size of the graph), the *temperature* parameter is periodically reduced by a preset constant factor d $\in (0, 1)$, and the algorithm iterates until this temperature reaches zero.

- The valuation of a layout is penalised if:
  - *Node overlap:* the distance between two distinct nodes is zero;
  - *Lack of gap:* the x-coordinates x_1 and x_2 of two unconnected nodes are too close, i.e., $|x_1 - x_2| < 1$;
  - *Long edges:* the distance between two edges is greater than an ideal.

- The *tweak* function takes a layout and a temperature and produces a new layout by making a series of random changes; each point in the graph may be changed to another point of the same type (left/right-facing). The number of such changes is dependent on the temperature, with higher temperatures giving rise to more changes. Hence, tweaking becomes more subtle as the algorithm progresses.

There are two features of the algorithm worthy of comment:

1. The temperature is kept fixed for a number of iterations which is some preset constant $c > 0$ times the temperature before being reduced. Thus, the number of iterations carried out at a given temperature decreases exponentially with the temperature.

2. There is randomness incorporated into the algorithm in that the layout may be randomly replaced by a less-optimal layout; however, the likelihood of this diminishes exponentially with the temperature and the poorness of the layout compared to the currently-identified best.

Figure 1 shows the results of applying our simulated annealing. The first layout in the figure is the ideal layout, whilst the following three illustrate progressive results. The unreadable labels are immaterial; all that is of interest is the layout.

For this run, we set the temperature decay $d = 0.75$ and the iteration constant $c = 3$; and used the following penalties in scoring: each node overlap and lack of gap is penalised -1; and each edge greater than 1 is penalised -10. As is apparent, the algorithm effectively works from a poor layout towards ones close to the ideal (though flipped vertically).

3.2   Verification: Insights from Failure

When verification tools discover a problem (such as the possibility of a crash), they can evidence the problem by providing a sequence of events leading from the initial configuration to the problematic state. However, being derived from a proof tool, this sequence is often provided in a mathematical language that is unnatural for signal engineers.

To overcome this, we have implemented an approach to visualising these traces in the OnTrack toolset [22]. The last image in Fig. 2 shows one way to depict a possible error state. Each step in the mathematical trace (i.e., each event causing a system state change) is shown through highlighting the state of the track plan elements. Users then have the option to step through each system state leading to the error.

For short traces, this approach can be sufficient. However, counterexample traces can easily become thousands of steps long with many of the steps being superfluous to what is actually causing the problem. We have thus provided users with a simple drop-down filter that allows them to select which types of key frames to present, specifically frames that correspond to particular events in the trace. For selection criteria, we include events from the generated trace. These include events like "route set" or "point switched position". Figure 2 shows an example of applying a filter that only shows "route set" events.

4   Expert Feedback

Four experts evaluated our tool and provided feedback (via interviews of approximately 30–45 min). Participants consisted of railway engineers working as safety

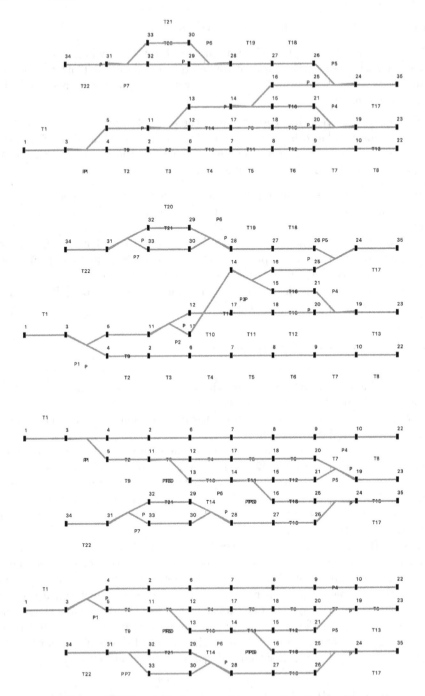

Fig. 1. Sample results from applying simulated annealing.

test engineers in industry (*P1* and *P4*), and academics working on applying formal methods to railways (*P2* and *P3*). The participants were asked to provide feedback on:

- The usefulness of the automatic layout when importing existing railway data. Participants were given a demonstration of our simulated annealing approach and example layouts. They were then asked to compare the automatic layouts to existing practice and to rate the usefulness from 1 (not useful) to 5 (highly useful) as a step towards the end goal of formal verification.
- The usefulness of the visualisation of counterexamples. Participants were presented with a counterexample trace and a demonstration of key event selection. They discussed the key events they would like to see and how useful an approach it would be.

4.1   Importation of Data and Automated Layout

The participants working in academia were keen on the approach, with average ratings: *General usefulness* 4; *Usefulness as a starting point for re-drawing* 3; and *Usefulness for verification* 5.

Clear layouts take precedence over geography. *P2* provides statements to support this idea: *"When verifying, you do not care too much about locations; but having a clear representation helps a lot in identifying errors"*. Similarly *P3* noted: *"I don't really care about the physical reality of the situation as long as I have the logic in place, that is perfect for me."* There is evidence that the automatic layout would have an impact on work practices, with *P2* noting the approach would *"save a lot of manual work"* and *P3* stating it is a *"good way to share benchmarks for verification without spending time encoding"*.

However, *P3* cautioned using automatic layout as a starting point for editing as it may lead to human errors: *"Human error may be a problem if the plan is laid out automatically and doesn't match the real-life model"*. *P2* noted that it would be useful to *"set a region as a 'correct' part of the plan before re-applying, so that you eventually get a plan that corresponds to the real plan"*. This indicates that we should use actual geographic information when available.

The participants working within the railway industry on average rated automatic layout as follows: *General usefulness* 3; *Usefulness as a starting point for re-drawing* 3.5; and *Usefulness for verification* 4. These participants noted that the usefulness depends on company specific formats versus shared data. *P4* noted: *"It could be very useful for some things but not for others; If you don't have the original scheme plan, it would be very useful."*

P1 stated that the approach would be more useful if it provided affordances for user steering or manipulation of the layout, particularly for point directions. From these participants, it is clear that if we have existing track layout information we should use it, but that the automatic layout tool can be useful when this information is not present.

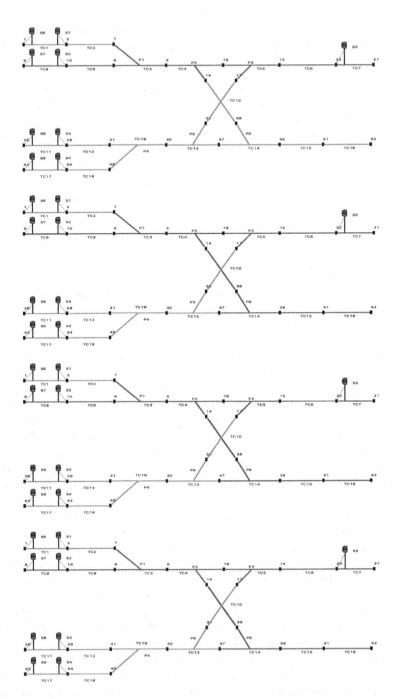

Fig. 2. Presentation of an error trace using the "route set" filter. Green indicates a set route, blue indicates occupation by a train, red an issue, here a "run through". (Color figure online)

4.2   Counterexample Visualisation

With respect to visualising counterexample traces, the feedback was positive. Academics gave the following average ratings: *General usefulness of step function* 4.5; and *Dynamic selection of key frames* 4.5. Industry engineers gave the following average ratings: *General usefulness of step function* 4.5; and *Dynamic selection of key frames* 4.5.

P1 noted that the implemented visual approach was in line with their mental model when performing a trace and would save time: *"This is what I do now but without the visual assistance, which would make it quicker"*. All bar one participant explicitly stated that they would like to have all counterexample steps available as well as key frame selection. *P3* stated: *"I think you need both the full trace and be able to jump between states; over simplification doesn't always make things easier"*. Interestingly, participants agreed that key frames would be very useful for experienced users, but a full trace would help for novice users. For example, *P2* noted: *"I think it depends on experience: senior verification engineers may identify problems using only a few key frames, but younger people may like to see the full trace to help understanding"*. *P3* noted: *"Advanced verification experts could look at brief traces and likely detect problems"*. All participants also agreed that the most vital key frame would be "route setting" as described by *P4*: *"Route setting will highlight where the error is in the control table."*

Participants suggested improvements, with three participants saying that viewing detail in time around a particular key frame would be useful. *P1* stated: *"It may be an option to have few of them, maybe 4-5 before and after an event"*. Similarly, *P2* and *P3* would like to see events within an area of a scheme plan, with *P3* stating: *"I might like to see all steps within a particular section."*

5   Conclusion

We have presented a technique that increases the accessibility and usability of formal methods within the railway verification community. Our solution consists of two parts. Firstly, we apply simulated annealing to automatically lay out railway graphs when no geographic information is available, improving interoperability between railway data sets. Secondly, we present key frame visualisations to support the understanding of counterexamples as presented in the language of the domain. Both approaches have been evaluated by expert users.

In future work, we would like to follow up on feedback from expert users and use small multiples [28] to visualise details (i.e., nearby frames) around key frames of interest. Similarly, we would like to explore the application of simulated annealing within subgraphs of a railway graph. To this end, constraint-based methods [9,10] could be useful. Finally, we would like to perform more formal evaluations of the railway layout algorithm through metric experiments as well as user studies on realistic tasks that railway engineers are required to perform on a regular basis.

Acknowledgments. The authors wish to thank Siemens Rail Automation UK, in particular Simon Chadwick, Mark Thomas and Thomas Werner for their support in undertaking this work.

References

1. Aber, N., Blanc, B., Ferkane, N., Meziani, M., Ordioni, J.: RBS2HLL. In: Collart-Dutilleul, S., Lecomte, T., Romanovsky, A. (eds.) RSSRail 2019. LNCS, vol. 11495, pp. 191–201. Springer, Cham (2019). https://doi.org/10.1007/978-3-030-18744-6_12
2. Archambault, D., Purchase, H.C.: Can animation support the visualization of dynamic graphs? Inf. Sci. **330**, 495–509 (2016)
3. Archambault, D., Purchase, H.C.: On the effective visualisation of dynamic attribute cascades. Inf. Vis. **15**(1), 51–63 (2016)
4. Barsky, A., Munzner, T., Gardy, J., Kincaid, R.: Cerebral: visualizing multiple experimental conditions on a graph with biological context. IEEE Trans. Vis. Comput. Graph. **14**(6), 1253–1260 (2008)
5. Beck, F., Burch, M., Diehl, S., Weiskopf, D.: A taxonomy and survey of dynamic graph visualization. Comput. Graph. Forum **36**(1), 133–159 (2017)
6. Bernardeschi, C., Fantechi, A., Gnesi, S., Mongardi, G.: Proving safety properties for embedded control systems. In: Hlawiczka, A., Silva, J.G., Simoncini, L. (eds.) EDCC 1996. LNCS, vol. 1150, pp. 321–332. Springer, Heidelberg (1996). https://doi.org/10.1007/3-540-61772-8_46
7. Brandes, U., Wagner, D.: Using graph layout to visualize train interconnection data. In: Whitesides, S.H. (ed.) GD 1998. LNCS, vol. 1547, pp. 44–56. Springer, Heidelberg (1998). https://doi.org/10.1007/3-540-37623-2_4
8. Davidson, R., Harel, D.: Drawing graphs nicely using simulated annealing. ACM Trans. Graph. **15**(4), 301–331 (1996)
9. Dwyer, T.: Scalable, versatile and simple constrained graph layout. Comput. Graph. Forum **28**(3), 991–998 (2009)
10. Dwyer, T., Koren, Y., Marriott, K.: IPSep-CoLa: an incremental procedure for separation constraint layout of graphs. IEEE Trans. Vis. Comput. Graph. **12**(5), 821–828 (2006)
11. Eisner, C.: Using symbolic model checking to verify the railway stations of Hoorn-Kersenboogerd and Heerhugowaard. In: Pierre, L., Kropf, T. (eds.) CHARME 1999. LNCS, vol. 1703, pp. 99–109. Springer, Heidelberg (1999). https://doi.org/10.1007/3-540-48153-2_9
12. Ferrari, A., Fantechi, A., Gnesi, S., Magnani, G.: Model-based development and formal methods in the railway industry. IEEE Softw. **30**(3), 28–34 (2013)
13. Ferrari, A., Magnani, G., Grasso, D., Fantechi, A.: Model checking interlocking control tables. In: Schnieder, E., Tarnai, G. (eds.) FORMS/FORMAT 2010. Springer, Berlin (2011). https://doi.org/10.1007/978-3-642-14261-1_11
14. Fokkink, W., Hollingshead, P.: Verification of interlockings: from control tables to ladder logic diagrams. In: FMICS 1998. CWI (1998)
15. Groote, J.F., van Vlijmen, S., Koorn, J.: The safety guaranteeing system at station hoorn-kersenboogerd. Technical report, Utrecht University (1995)
16. Haxthausen, A.E., Peleska, J., Pinger, R.: Applied bounded model checking for interlocking system designs. In: Counsell, S., Núñez, M. (eds.) SEFM 2013. LNCS, vol. 8368, pp. 205–220. Springer, Cham (2014). https://doi.org/10.1007/978-3-319-05032-4_16

17. Idani, A., Ledru, Y., Ait Wakrime, A., Ben Ayed, R., Bon, P.: Towards a tool-based domain specific approach for railway systems modeling and validation. In: Collart-Dutilleul, S., Lecomte, T., Romanovsky, A. (eds.) RSSRail 2019. LNCS, vol. 11495, pp. 23–40. Springer, Cham (2019). https://doi.org/10.1007/978-3-030-18744-6_2

18. Iliasov, A., Taylor, D., Laibinis, L., Romanovsky, A.: SAFECOMP 2018 (2018)

19. James, P.: Sat-based model checking and its applications to train control software. Master's thesis, Swansea University (2010)

20. James, P., et al.: Verification of solid state interlocking programs. In: Counsell, S., Núñez, M. (eds.) SEFM 2013. LNCS, vol. 8368, pp. 253–268. Springer, Cham (2014). https://doi.org/10.1007/978-3-319-05032-4_19

21. James, P., Roggenbach, M.: Encapsulating formal methods within domain specific languages: a solution for verifying railway scheme plans. Math. Comput. Sci. 8(1), 11–38 (2014). https://doi.org/10.1007/s11786-014-0174-0

22. James, P., Trumble, M., Treharne, H., Roggenbach, M., Schneider, S.: OnTrack: an open tooling environment for railway verification. In: Brat, G., Rungta, N., Venet, A. (eds.) NFM 2013. LNCS, vol. 7871, pp. 435–440. Springer, Heidelberg (2013). https://doi.org/10.1007/978-3-642-38088-4_30

23. Kamada, T., Kawai, S.: An algorithm for drawing general undirected graphs. Inf. Process. Lett. 31(1), 7–15 (1989)

24. Kanso, K., Moller, F., Setzer, A.: Verification of safety properties in railway interlocking systems defined with ladder logic. In: AVOCS08. Glasgow University (2008)

25. Macedo, H.D., Fantechi, A., Haxthausen, A.E.: Compositional model checking of interlocking systems for lines with multiple stations. In: Barrett, C., Davies, M., Kahsai, T. (eds.) NFM 2017. LNCS, vol. 10227, pp. 146–162. Springer, Cham (2017). https://doi.org/10.1007/978-3-319-57288-8_11

26. Nöllenburg, M.: A survey on automated metro map layout methods. In: Schematic Mapping Workshop (2014)

27. Parillaud, C., Fonteneau, Y., Belmonte, F.: Interlocking formal verification at alstom signalling. In: Collart-Dutilleul, S., Lecomte, T., Romanovsky, A. (eds.) RSSRail 2019. LNCS, vol. 11495, pp. 215–225. Springer, Cham (2019). https://doi.org/10.1007/978-3-030-18744-6_14

28. Tufte, E.: Envisioning Information. Graphics Press, Cheshire (1990)

29. Tversky, B., Morrison, J., Betrancourt, M.: Animation: can it facilitate? Int. J. Hum.-Comput. Stud. 57(4), 247–262 (2002)

30. Wolff, A.: Drawing subway maps: a survey. Informatik - Forschung und Entwicklung 22(1), 23–44 (2007). https://doi.org/10.1007/s00450-007-0036-y

31. Wu, H.-Y., Niedermann, B., Takahashi, S., Nöllenburg, V.: A survey on computing schematic network maps: the challenge to interactivity. In: The 2nd Schematic Mapping Workshop, Vienna, Austria (2018)

Probabilistic Activity Recognition for Serious Games with Applications in Medicine

Elisabetta De Maria[1], Thibaud L'Yvonnet[2(✉)], Sabine Moisan[2], and Jean-Paul Rigault[2]

[1] Université Côte d'Azur, CNRS, I3S, Nice, France
edemaria@i3s.unice.fr
[2] Université Côte d'Azur, INRIA Sophia Antipolis, Nice, France
{thibaud.lyvonnet,sabine.moisan,jean-paul.rigault}@inria.fr

Abstract. Human activity recognition plays an important role especially in medical applications. This paper proposes a formal approach to model such activities, taking into account possible variations in human behavior. Starting from an activity description enriched with event occurrence probabilities, we translate it into a corresponding formal model based on discrete-time Markov chains (DTMCs). We use the PRISM framework and its model checking facilities to express and check interesting temporal logic properties (PCTL) concerning the dynamic evolution of activities. We illustrate our approach on the model of a *serious game* used by clinicians to monitor Alzheimer patients. We expect that such a modeling approach could provide new indications for interpreting patient performances. This paper addresses only the model definition and its suitability to check behavioral properties of interest. Indeed, this is mandatory before envisioning any clinical study.

Keywords: Activity description · Probabilistic model · Model checking · Serious games · Bio-medicine

1 Introduction

In the last decades human behavior recognition has become a crucial research axis [25] and is employed in many contexts, such as visual surveillance in public places [6,20], smart homes [26], or pedestrian detection for smart cars [9,24]. A recent application in the health domain are "serious games", used to evaluate the performances of patients affected by neuro-degenerative pathologies such as the Alzheimer disease [23]. Behavior, emotions, and performance displayed by patients during these games can give indications on their disease.

A lot has been done, especially in computer vision, on simple *action* recognition [27], whereas we target complex *activities*, including several actions. In our view, an activity consists in a set of scenarios that describe possible behavioral variants. Therefore, recognition means to identify which scenario is running from

© Springer Nature Switzerland AG 2020
O. Hasan and F. Mallet (Eds.): FTSCS 2019, CCIS 1165, pp. 106–124, 2020.
https://doi.org/10.1007/978-3-030-46902-3_7

inputs produced by different types of sensors. Currently, we mostly use video cameras but also binary sensors or audio signals. Our ultimate aim is to propose a general (human) activity recognition system that helps medical practitioners in monitoring patients with cognitive deficiencies.

All the scenarios of an activity are not equivalent: some are typical (thus frequent) while others seldom happen; this is due to variations in the behavior of the actors involved in the activity. To improve the analysis and interpretation of an activity (e.g., a patient playing a serious game), we propose to quantify the likelihood of these variations by associating probabilities with the key actions of the activity description. The recognition process remains deterministic since, at recognition time, only one scenario at a time will be played and recognized.

Our first contribution is a formal modeling framework where activities are represented by (hierarchical) discrete-time Markov chains whose edges can be decorated with probabilities. Markov chains are deterministic and do not impose to associate a real duration with each action, contrary to, e.g., timed automata. We can thus "master" the time in our activity models, restricting it to the instants when some significant events occur, hence reducing the duration of simulations or model checking. Furthermore, in the games that we address we can have non homogeneous delays between actions and we do not want to consider the smallest delay as the (minimal) time unit, since that would generate a huge number of states in the model and model checking would not be feasible. Our choice for using formal modeling and model checking is mainly motivated by their ability to directly provide probabilities associated with *classes* of paths and to test universal properties on the model, contrary to simulation techniques which only deal with existential properties.

As a second contribution, we have implemented discrete-time Markov chains using the PRISM language [15]. We used temporal logic to encode some relevant properties on their dynamical evolution, and we applied model checking techniques [8] to automatically validate the models with respect to these properties and to infer the probabilities of some interesting paths. When applied to the recognition of serious games for Alzheimer patients, this technique can provide medical doctors with indications to interpret patients' performance.

We are developing a language for hospital practitioners to describe activities they expect from their patients as programs representing all the envisioned paths (possible combinations of actions from the patient or the environment), both typical behaviors and marginal ones. Some actions will be performed for sure by the patient (or the environment) and need no probabilities. Other ones depend on the stage of Alzheimer of the patient. With these latter actions, practitioners can associate a discrete probability level (e.g., low, medium, high...) or directly a real number or weight. Hence, we can deduce how relevant the scenario played by a patient is. For example, if a patient known to be healthy plays a "medium cognition deficit" scenario, our system is able to spot this information. The same goes if a "severe cognition deficit" patient plays a "healthy" scenario.

Before performing clinical tests on real patients, it is necessary to validate our approach and to explore the kind of properties that model checking can achieve, which is the focus of this paper.

The paper is organized as follows. Section 2 formally details discrete-time Markov chains and their support in the PRISM model checker. Section 3 presents a serious game case study used as a running example. Section 4 introduces the PRISM encoding of this game as a discrete-time Markov chain and Sect. 5 applies model checking to it. Finally, Sect. 6 concludes and opens future research directions.

2   The PRISM Model Checker

Several Probabilistic model checkers exist (such as Uppaal [4] or PAT [22]). We decided to rely on PRISM [15], developed as a probabilistic model checker since the beginning and well established in the literature. More precisely, PRISM is a tool for formal modeling and analysis of systems with random or probabilistic behavior. It has already been used to describe human activity [21]. It supports several types of probabilistic models, discrete as well as continuous. In this work we rely on discrete-time Markov chains (DTMC), which are transition systems augmented with probabilities. Their set of states represents the possible configurations of the system being modeled, and the transitions between states represent the evolution of the system, which occurs in discrete-time steps. Probabilities to transit between states are given by discrete probability distributions. Markov chains are memoryless, that is, their current state contains all the information needed to compute future states. More precisely:

Definition 1. *A Discrete-Time Markov Chain over a set of atomic propositions AP is a tuple (S, S_{init}, P, L) where S is a set of states (state space), $S_{init} \subseteq S$ is the set of initial states, $P : S \times S \to [0, 1]$ is the transition probability function (where $\sum_{s' \in S} P(s, s') = 1$ for all $s \in S$), and $L : S \to 2^{AP}$ is a function labeling states with atomic propositions over AP.*

An example of DTMC of a simple two-state game is depicted in Fig. 1. In this game, the player has to press a button as many times as she wishes.

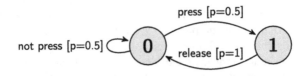

Fig. 1. DTMC representing a simple press button game. Each edge is labelled with both an action and the corresponding probability.

2.1 PRISM Modeling Language

PRISM provides a state-based modeling language inspired from the reactive modules formalism of [2]. A model is composed of a set of *modules* which can interact with each other. The state of a module is given by the values of its *local variables* and the global state of the whole model is determined by the local states of all its modules. The dynamics of each module is described by a set of commands of the form: [ ]*guard* → *prob*$_1$: *update*$_1$ + ... + *prob*$_n$: *update*$_n$; where *guard* is a predicate over all the variables of the model, corresponding to a condition to be verified in order to execute the command, and each *update* indicates a possible transition of the model, achieved by giving new values to variables. Each *update* is assigned a probability and, for each command, the sum of probabilities must be 1. The square brackets at the beginning of each command can either be empty or contain labels representing *actions*. These actions can be used to force two or more modules to transit simultaneously. The PRISM code for the DTMC of Fig. 1 is shown in Algorithm 1. In this code, the unique integer variable y represents the state of the player, it ranges over $\{0, 1\}$. Its initial value is 0. When the guard $y = 0$ is true, the updates $(y' = 0)$ and $(y' = 1)$ and their associated probabilities state that the value of y remains at 0 with probability 0.5 and switches to 1 with probability 0.5. When $y = 1$, the update $(y' = 0)$ with probability 1 states that y switches back to 0.

Finally, PRISM models can be extended with *rewards* [16], associating real values with model states or transitions. An example of reward is given at the end of Algorithm 1: each time $y = 1$ (button pressed), the reward is incremented.

Algorithm 1. PRISM code for Figure 1 DTMC.

```
dtmc //Discrete-Time Markov Chain
module good_answer_game
y: [0..1] init 0;
//Commands
[ ] y=0 -> 0.5:(y'=0) + 0.5:(y'=1); // y' corresponds to y in the next instant
[ ] y=1 -> 1:(y'=0);
endmodule
rewards "y"
y=1: 1;
endrewards
```

2.2 Probabilistic Temporal Logic

The dynamics of DTMCs can be specified in PRISM thanks to the PCTL (Probabilistic Computation Tree Logic) temporal logic [11]. PCTL extends the CTL logic (Computation Tree Logic) [8] with probabilities. The following state quantifiers are available in PCTL: **X** (next time), **F** (sometimes in the future), **G** (always in the future), and **U** (until). Note that the classical path quantifiers **A** (forall) and **E** (exist) of CTL are replaced by probabilities. Thus, instead of saying that some property holds for all paths or for some paths, we say that a property holds for a certain fraction of the paths [11]. The most important operator in PCTL is **P**, which allows to reason about the probability of event occurrences. As an example, the PCTL property P= 0.5 [X (y = 1)] holds in a state if the probability that $y = 1$ is true in the next state equals 0.5. All the state quantifiers given above, with the exception of **X**, have bounded variants, where a time bound is imposed on the property. Furthermore, in order to compute the actual probability that some behavior of a model occurs, the **P** operator can take the form P=?. For instance, the property P =? [G (y = 0)] expresses the probability that y always equals 0.

PRISM also supports properties on the expected values of rewards. The **R** operator allows to retrieve reward values. Additional operators have been introduced to deal with rewards: we mainly use **C** (cumulative-reward). The property C<=t corresponds to the reward accumulated along a path until t time units have elapsed. PRISM provides model checking algorithms [8] to automatically validate DTMCs over PCTL properties and reward-based ones. On demand, the algorithms compute the actual probability of some behavior of a model to occur.

3   Motivation and Case Study

For non experts in computer science, we propose a language to describe activities to recognize in real-time. It offers usual instructions such as parallel execution, conditional, or repetition. Most instructions may have associated weights in the form of real numbers between 0 and 1 or using a discrete scale. These weights will be digitized (if they are discrete) and normalized to obtain probabilities. In this paper we do not provide a full description of the language, which is still under development, but we simply illustrate its use with an example of a serious game (see listing 1.1).

Serious games constitute a domain in which real-time activity recognition is particularly relevant: the expected behavior is well identified and it is possible to rely on different sensors (biometric and external) while playing the game. In the health domain, they can be used to incite patients to practice physical exercises [7], to train medical staff with engaging activities [5], or to help diagnose and treat patients [3,10]. When formally modeling a diagnosis game, a user can associate probabilities with instructions to represent a healthy or a pathological behavior. These probabilities are initially defined according to physicians past experience. Properties can then be written to extract relevant data, to be compared first, with experimental results in order to refine the model and ultimately, with real patients results.

After discussions with medical doctors, we identified three prospective uses for our approach:

– *Evaluate a patient.* If a patient comes for the first time to get a diagnosis, we can compare her results to a reference model representing a "healthy" patient behavior. Our approach gives us a fairly good idea of what such a healthy behavior is, as for example, the approximate number of good and bad answers at the end or at a certain point of the game, the type of errors made, or the probability for the patient to quit the game before its end. If the patient's results differ too much from the simulation results, it may be due to a disease and the patient might need a full diagnosis from a doctor.

– *Monitor a patient.* For a given patient, a customized profile can be created according to the results obtained during the first tests. Thus, from one session to the next, her health improvement or deterioration could be monitored. If the ratio of good/bad answers is increasing while the number of answered questions is not decreasing, it may show an improvement. On the other hand, if the ratio is decreasing or if the number of answered questions is decreasing, it may show that the disease is progressing.

– *Create a cohort of patients.* Once a reference profile is validated, we can use it to determine whether a new group of patients belongs to this specific category. This process is similar to a screening test on a population as it would only be a step before a definitive diagnosis; it is cheaper compared to a full diagnosis for the whole population and faster thanks to the automation of the process. For example, such tests will allow practitioners to shortlist patients to apply a specific protocol on this cohort.

3.1   Case Study

As a use case, we consider a serious game to analyze the behavior of Alzheimer patients: the *Match Items game* [23]. In this game, patients interact with a touch-pad. They are asked to match a random picture displayed in the center of the touch-pad with the corresponding element in a list of pictures (see Fig. 2).

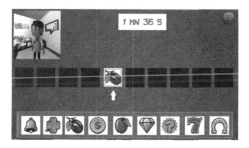

Fig. 2. Display of the Match Items game.

If the patient chooses the right picture, a happy smiley is displayed and a new picture is proposed. Otherwise a sad smiley is displayed and the patient is asked to try again. If the patient does not interact quickly enough with the touch-pad (more than 10 s of inactivity), the game prompts her to choose a picture. Whenever the patient exits the game zone, the game is aborted. The game lasts at most five minutes. A simplified pseudo-code program describing this game is given in Listing 1.1.

Initial: patient inside game_zone and patient presses_start_button
  during 300s
    console displays_picture
    when [0.0005] patient exits game_zone
    preempt { emit no_player; exit }
      // *main loop on each occurrence of the asks_ to_ choose event*
      every console asks_to_choose patient
        switch
        case [0.75] (patient selects_picture)
          // *patient selected something*
          switch
          case [0.66] (console displays_happy_smiley)
            // *correct answer: new picture and continue loop*
            console displays_picture !! *count: happy_ smileys*
          case [0.33] (console displays_sad_smiley)
            // *wrong answer: loop keeping current picture*
            nothing !! *count: sad_ smileys*
          end switch
        case [0.25] (console notifies_inactivity)
          // *patient did not react, continue with same picture*
          nothing !! *count: non_ interactions*
        end switch
      end every
    end when
  end during
emit game_over

Listing 1.1. Serious game pseudo code description.

The game starts when the patient has been detected in the game zone and presses the start button. The **when** clause introduces a preemption: the game may abort prematurely, whatever its execution state is, if the patient leaves the game zone before the normal end of the game; this is possible with Alzheimer patients who may suffer from attention deficiency. The core of the game is described via the probabilistic **switch cases**. The branches of a **switch** are exclusive and their order is a priority order: the first branch whose awaited event occurs executes its statements. A probability of occurrence may be associated with a branch (indicated within square brackets in the pseudo-code).

Furthermore, the clinicians can indicate (through *!!* comments) significant events that should be remembered and counted. For instance, the number of happy smileys displayed during the game gives an interesting information about a patient's performance. Note that, in this example, the sum of the weights in the probabilistic switch case and in the preemptive condition is not 1. A normalization will be applied to obtain the probabilities for the formal model. Thus, the user does not have to bother with numeric computations.

4   Serious Game Model

We model the behavior of a patient in this game using a discrete-time Markov chain (DTMC). To the best of our knowledge, DTMC models are barely used for the description of human behavior, although we can cite [12]. In computer vision, Hidden Markov Models (HMMs) are a popular approach for the description of activities [1,13]. However, PRISM and most of the other probabilistic model checkers do not allow to check temporal logic properties over HMMs.

Due to a limitation in PRISM, we explicitly represent all the possible states in the model. This limitation concerns looping through a state: in PRISM Markov chains, we cannot put a limit on the number of times we can loop through a state. This means that, even if we give a low probability to the loop transition, there will always be a risk for a simulation to never quit this loop (fairness is not automatically imposed). By explicitly representing all possible states of the game, we avoid this issue. Since the game activity lasts at most five minutes (or three-hundred seconds), we know that there will be a finite number of states in our chain. Thus, in the PRISM model, we made the assumption that a patient needs at least three seconds to select a picture (minimum time needed to think of which picture to choose and to touch the screen to select it).

4.1   Model Design

With the previous assumption, we can translate the time constraint of three-hundred seconds in a maximum number of actions (or events) that can happen in a scenario. If the patient keeps on selecting pictures, a smiley (happy or sad) is displayed. We call this event *selection* and it cannot happen more than a hundred times in a row ($300/3 = 100$). On the other hand, if the patient does not interact with the game for ten seconds, the system displays a message (event *notifies_inactivity* in listing 1.1). We call this event *inactivity* and it cannot happen more than thirty times in a row ($300/10 = 30$).

To represent all combinations of these two events, we picture a right-angle triangle (Fig. 3a). The edge of length one hundred (representing the scenario of a succession of *selection*) and the edge of length thirty (representing the scenario of a succession of *inactivity*) form the perpendicular sides of the triangle. Each state of this triangle, except those on the hypotenuse, have three different possible transitions, represented in Fig. 3b.

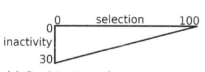

(a) Combinations of events triangle.

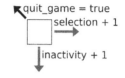

(b) Possible state transitions for states symbolizing the game session.

Fig. 3. Concepts of the model of activity.

According to Fig. 3b, a state can either increment *selection* and move on the *selection* axis, or increment *inactivity* and move on the *inactivity* axis. To represent the action of the patient leaving the game before the end of the five minutes (which could be detected by a camera) we use a Boolean variable called *quit_game*. If this variable is true, the state previously reached in the triangle is considered as the final state of the game session.

All states on the hypotenuse represent the end of the five minutes of the game. The only possible transition from them is equivalent to *quit_game*.

4.2   PRISM Implementation

The model is composed of a single module called "Serious_game"[1]. In this module, the location of the patient is represented by an integer variable with range [0..2] called *location*: 0 represents the patient being in the room before playing, 1 the patient being in the gaming area, and 2 the patient being outside this area.

As previously described, the interaction of a patient with the game is represented as an integer variable with range [0..100] called *selection*. A value i represents the fact that the patient had i interaction(s) with the game.

The event of the game displaying a message after ten seconds of inactivity is represented as an integer variable with range [0..30] called *inactivity*. A value i represents the fact that the game displayed the message i time(s).

To ease readability and re-usability of the module, each of the previous variables gets its maximum value defined outside the module in a global variable: *location_max*, *selection_max* and *inactivity_max*, respectively.

The variables *selection_max* and *inactivity_max* are also used to determine if a state belongs to the hypotenuse of the triangle mentioned before. To do so, we solve the following equation (where $\lceil x \rceil$ is the application of the ceiling function to x, denoting the smallest integer greater or equal to x):

$$inactivity = \left\lceil \left(-\frac{inactivity\_max}{selection\_max} \right) \times action + inactivity\_max \right\rceil \qquad (1)$$

To take advantage of the rewards of PRISM, we use Boolean variables to represent the other concepts.

- The event "a happy (resp., sad) smiley is displayed" for a good (resp., bad) answer is represented by the variable *happy_smiley* (resp., *sad_smiley*).
- The event "the patient leaves the game area before the end of the five minutes" is represented by *quit_game*.
- The event "the console displays a message after ten seconds of inactivity" is represented by *non_interaction*.

Only one of these variables at a time can be *true*. Each time a variable is *true*, it means that the event it represents happened and the associated reward is incremented. The rewards associated with these Boolean variables are the

---

[1] PRISM code at https://gitlab.com/ThibLY/activity-recognition-modeling.

following: *happy_smiley* is associated with *Happy_smiley_reward*, *sad_smiley* with *Sad_smiley_reward*, *non_interaction* with *Non_interaction_reward*, and *quit_game* with *Leave_game_reward*; the amount of time spent in the game by the patient is represented by *Gaming_time*.

The *Gaming_time* reward is more complex than the others because it increases by three units for each good or bad answer and by ten units for each inactivity message displayed by the console.

The state of the patient can go through different transitions only if it matches one of the four different guards of the "Serious_game" module:

1. variable *location* is equal to 0, meaning the patient is in the room;
2. variable *location* is equal to 1, *time_Is_Not_Over* is *true* and *quit_game* is *false*, meaning the patient is playing the game;
3. variable *location* is equal to 1 and *time_Is_Over* is *true*, meaning the patient has played for the maximum time;
4. variable *location* is equal to 1 and *quit_game* is *true*, meaning the patient left the game before the end of the maximum duration.

The PRISM code for the command associated with the second guard is given in Listing 1.2, where $p1 = 0.5/sum$, $p2 = 0.25/sum$, $p3 = 0.25/sum$, and $p4 = 0.0005/sum$, with $sum = 0.5 + 0.25 + 0.25 + 0.0005$.

```
[acts] location=1 & !time_Is_Over & quit_game=false ->
    // good answer
    p1 : (selection'=selection+1) & (happy_smiley'=true) &
          (sad_smiley'=false) & (inactivity_bool'=false) +
    // bad answer
    p2 : (selection'=selection+1) & (happy_smiley'=false) &
          (sad_smiley'=true) & (inactivity_bool'=false) +
    // inactivity
    p3 : (inactivity'=inactivity+1) & (happy_smiley'=false)&
          (sad_smiley'=false) & (inactivity_bool'=true) +
    // game left
    p4 : (quit_game'=true) & (happy_smiley'=false) &
          (sad_smiley'=false) & (inactivity_bool'=false);
```

Listing 1.2. Excerpt from the Serious_Game module.

The global variable *time_Is_Over* is defined to ease the readability of the module. It contains a Boolean expression to determine if the maximum number of actions that a patient can perform is reached.

The state transitions performed in a simulation describe the patient's behavior in a scenario. Some of these transitions have attached probabilities. The different possible transitions for a patient are the following:

– if the first guard is *true*, *location* is updated to 1, meaning the patient enters the gaming area;

- if the second guard is *true*, four different transitions can be taken with different probabilities: (i) the patient gives a good answer (with a weight of 0.5 for our tests); (ii) the patient gives a bad answer (weight 0.25); (iii) the system asks the patient to choose a picture after ten seconds of inactivity (weight 0.25); (iv) the patient leaves the game (weight 0.0005);
- if the third or fourth guard is *true*, *location* is updated to 2, meaning the patient leaves the gaming area.

In the following section, as a theoretical example, we will assume that these parameters represent a typical patient with mild cognitive impairment (MCI).

5   Temporal Logic Properties and Results

In the previous model, we encoded and tested several properties in PCTL. The tests were run on a computer with eight processors (Intel(R) Core(TM) i7-7820HQ CPU @ 2.90 GHz) and 32 GB RAM, running under the Fedora Linux operating system.

Two kinds of properties may be defined: those to verify the model and those oriented toward the medical domain, which may give indications to a practitioner regarding a patient's behavior.

5.1   Model Verification

One typical property of the model itself is that all the model scenarios must reach the final state, which means that the variable *location* must eventually be updated to 2. The following property verifies that this update occurs:

Property 1. What is the probability to reach the final state of the Markov chain?

$$P =?[F \ (location = location\_max)]$$

If the result is below 1, there exists a possibility to never reach the final state. This possibility only occurs if there is an error in *Match Items game* model. In our case the result is 1.0; it is obtained in 0.002 s.

5.2   Medically Oriented Properties

Properties About Interactions. The following properties evaluate the probability for a path to go through i occurrences of *selection* and j occurrences of *inactivity*. The first three properties check the probability to end the game with $i = selection\_max$ or $j = inactivity\_max$ or i in between 0 and *selection_max* and j in between 0 and *inactivity_max*. The last property checks the probability to leave the game before the end of the five minutes.

Property 2. What is the probability for a patient to never interact with the game until the end of the duration of the game?

$$P =?[F \ (selection = 0) \ \& \ (inactivity = inactivity\_max)]$$

Property 3. What is the probability for a patient to interact with the game until the end of the game without any interruption?

$$P =?[F \ (selection = selection\_max) \ \& \ (inactivity = 0)]$$

Property 4. What is the probability for a patient to start the game and to interact with it forty-three times (not necessarily consecutively) and not to interact with it eighteen times (not necessarily consecutive)?

$$P =?[F \ (selection = 43) \ \& \ (inactivity = 18)]$$

Property 5. What is the probability for a patient to leave the game before the maximum game duration?

$$P =?[F \ (quit\_game = true)]$$

Discussion. The results for these properties are displayed in Table 1, together with their computing time.

Table 1. Results from Property 3 to 5.

Property	Result	Time (s)
Property 2	8.5445×10^{-19}	0.026
Property 3	3.0508×10^{-13}	0.049
Property 4	2.3188×10^{-2}	0.03
Property 5	3.1364×10^{-2}	0.058

The probability obtained for Property 2 is rather low. This is due to the fact that there is only one path leading to the state satisfying this property. Moreover, this path only goes through low probability transitions.

Two observations can be made on the results of Property 3: (i) the probability is higher than the one of Property 2; (ii) this probability is low. The first observation is due to the fact that the transition taken and repeated when this property is verified has three times more chances to be taken over the one taken to satisfy Property 2. The probability of Property 3 is pretty low because there is only one path made of three hundred transitions that satisfies this property.

Property 4 checks the probability to reach one of the state representing the end of the five minutes of the game. To give an example, a state which can only be reached with paths composed of 43 transitions representing an interaction and 18 transitions representing a non-interaction was chosen. The probability for this property is higher than the one of Property 3. This is due to the fact that this state can be reached by a large amount of paths.

The probability obtained for Property 5 is approximately 3% even though the probability for the path to go through "*quit_game = true*" is five hundred times lower than the probability to take the non-interaction transition. To satisfy this property, all paths in which the transition *quit_game* is taken are considered. Note that, if one increases the maximum duration of the game but keeps the parameters of the model as they are, the result of Property 5 increases.

Possible Medical Significance. The results obtained from the above properties give several indications. In the case of a cohort selection based on this model, the behavior described in Property 4 and Property 5 should be observed quite rarely (respectively 2% and 3% of the cases). The behaviors described in Property 2 and Property 3 must not be observed. If a cohort differs too much on the frequency of these behaviors, the practitioners must discard or deeply change it. Otherwise, the risk to perform a clinical test on the wrong sample of population is too high.

Properties About Quality of Actions. These properties are relative to the quality of the actions that can be performed. The first one provides an average "score" for the model. The second and third ones give probabilities to follow some specific paths in the model.

Property 6. What is the average amount of good responses given by patients during their game sessions?

$$R\{``Happy\_smiley\_reward"\} =?[F\ (location = location\_max)]$$

Property 7. What is the probability for a patient to choose the correct picture exactly one time and to never choose a good one again until the end of the game?

$$P =?[(F\ happy\_smiley = true)\ \&\ (G\ ((happy\_smiley = true) =>$$
$$(X\ G\ happy\_smiley = false\ \&\ quit\_game = false)))]$$

Property 8. What is the probability for a patient to directly choose the right picture, without choosing a wrong picture before?

$$P =?[F\ (selection = 1\ \&\ happy\_smiley = true)]$$

Discussion. The results for these properties are displayed in Table 2a and 2b.

Table 2. Results for the properties concerning the quality of actions.

Reward	Result	Time(s)
Happy_smiley_reward	31	0.044
Sad_smiley_reward	15	0.019
Inactivity_bool_reward	15	0.042

(a) Results of Property 6.

Property	Result	Time(s)
7	3.3012×10^{-12}	2.046
8	6.6622×10^{-1}	0.007

(b) Results of Properties 7 and 8.

Property 6 can be written for *Happy_smiley_reward, Sad_smiley_reward* and for *Inactivity_bool_reward.* According to its results, the average "score" for a cohort of patients matching this model parameters should be 31 good answers for 15 bad answers and there should be 15 inactivity messages before the end of the session.

Property 7 was the longest one to compute. The complexity of this property comes from the nesting of G operators. Property 8 gives the biggest probability value compared to all others. Indeed, unlike Property 7, there is a huge amount of scenarios that can validate it.

Possible Medical Significance. Still in the case of a cohort pre-selection, the group of patients should obtain an average "score" similar to the one obtained in Property 6. If the score differs too much from this result, the cohort must be rejected. According to the result of Property 7, a patient from this group is not expected to choose only one right answer and then stay without exiting until the end of the game. On the other hand, according to the result of Property 8, in this same group, it should be common to observe patients choosing the right picture on the first try (66% of the cohort).

5.3   Cumulative Rewards and Simulations

This subsection gives an example of a property which shows the interest to perform simulations of the model. We use the PRISM "cumulative reward" facilities to track how the model accumulates rewards over time. Properties using rewards can include variables such as the one indicating the number of steps to perform before checking the reward. This variable allows the use of the "run experiments" feature of PRISM and the acquisition of graphs of results.

Property 9. What is the amount of happy smileys accumulated within i steps?

$$R\{``Happy\_smiley\_reward"\} =?[C <= i]$$

where i is the number of steps to perform before checking the reward. This property is reused for *Sad_smiley_reward, Inactivity_bool_reward, Gaming_time* and *Leave_game_reward.*

Fig. 4. Average model checking results for rewards related to good answers, bad answers, non-interaction, and game leaving behavior.

In Fig. 4, the rewards for good answers, bad answers, and non-interactions have a linear increase until they reach a plateau. The values reached by the rewards are the ones obtained in Property 6. The reward for the action of leaving the game is almost equal to zero. This is because this reward can be incremented only once in a run and that there is only 3% of the paths (see Property 5) where a patient may leave the game before its maximum duration.

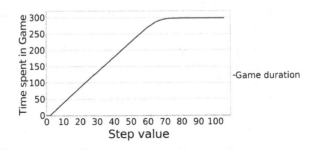

Fig. 5. Average duration of the game obtained with model checking.

In Fig. 5, the average game duration is slightly under 300 s. This is due to the paths where a patient may leave the game before the maximum duration. This shows that, although Eq. 1 in Sect. 4 implies an approximation with the ceiling function, the patients leaving the game are lowering the average enough to bring it just under the maximum expected value. As a final observation, the game duration reaches the plateau around the seventy-fifth step. This is due to the fact that most of the paths go through non-interaction transitions several times. Should they not go through these transitions at all, the plateau might have been reached around the 100th step.

In Fig. 6a, over 100 simulations, some of them (in blue/thin black in the figure) reach a maximum value which is above three-hundred seconds (still due to the approximation in Eq. 1). Among these 100 simulations, some do not reach 300 s, one of them (in red in Fig. 6a) even never increases and stays at 0. These simulations follow the paths where a modeled patient leaves the game before the

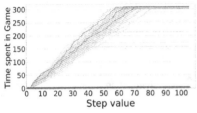

(a) Duration of the game over 100 runs.

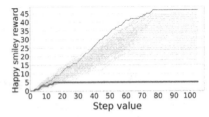

(b) Accumulation of good answers over 100 runs.

Fig. 6. Experiment results on the accumulation of rewards over 100 runs. (Color figure online)

end of the maximum duration. This experiment illustrates the results obtained with model checking (Property 5 and 6).

In Fig. 6, over the 100 simulations, the results present a high variability which cannot be foreseen with model checking. In this experiment, a maximum value of 47 good answers for a minimum of 5 good answers is reached.

Globally, in Fig. 6 as well as in Fig. 4, there is no "preferred" time to act during the game. This can be seen with the linear increase of each reward. This is due to the current version of the model; in fact, the states representing the game have homogeneous probabilities of transitions.

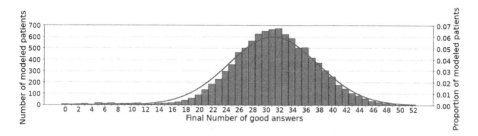

Fig. 7. Frequency of good answers over 10,000 runs (in blue/grey) and its fitting normal distribution with $\mu = 31.2131$ and $\sigma^2 = 43.9271$ (in red/black). (Color figure online)

Due to the difficulty to see the different runs in Fig. 6, a shell and a Python scripts were written to retrieve raw data from simulations. These data are used in Fig. 7 to display the frequency of good answers over 10,000 runs. In this figure, the distribution of the frequency of good answers at the end of the game can be approximated by a normal distribution of mean $\mu = 31.2131$. This result is coherent with the result of Property 2. It can be stated that a patient represented by this model is more likely to give around 31 good answers rather than 40 or 25 ones.

For medical doctors to use these results, a range of acceptance must be defined experimentally for the game. A patient supposedly represented by this model who gets results that are out of the range of acceptance can be interpreted in two different ways: Either the patient is not matching the model at all (improvement in the patient's behavior or wrong categorization of the patient) or the patient actually belongs to the group of patients represented by this model, but the model itself needs adjustments to better represent this group.

6   Conclusions and Future Work

In this paper, we target complex activity recognition, which remains a challenging research area [14] to obtain viable recognition systems. We propose a formal approach based on discrete-time Markov chains to model human activities. Important properties of such models can be automatically verified thanks to model checking. The technique we propose complements the main existing approaches in the field of activity recognition. Indeed, these approaches seldom address formal verification issues. Some work on human activity recognition relies on online model checking [17,18]. Probabilistic model checking can be used to debug activity models [19]. In our case, we use probabilities to explore paths associated with different behaviors.

Thanks to our formal probabilistic modelling approach we can expect three medically interesting outcomes. First, to evaluate a new patient before the first diagnosis of doctors, we can compare her game performance to a reference model representing a "healthy" behavior. Second, to monitor known patients, a customized model can be created according to their first results, and, over time, their health improvement or deterioration could be monitored. Finally, to preselect a cohort of patients, we can use a reference model to determine, in a fast way, whether a new group of patients belongs to this specific category.

Our models need to be updated according to real experiment results. When creating a reference model of a certain degree of Alzheimer disease, as for instance the "mild cognitive impairment", practitioners may initially configure it with probabilities deduced from their experience. This model will be verified and compared to the average results of several experiments done by a known population of "moderate cognitive deficits" patients. We will then use the results to adjust the model probabilities to obtain a more realistic model, providing a more accurate prediction.

As a first step, we encoded a serious game for Alzheimer patients as a DTMC in PRISM and we tested meaningful PCTL properties thanks to the PRISM model checker. These properties include the use of rewards to quantify the performances of patients.

The next step is to validate our approach as well as to test its scalability on three other serious games selected with the help of clinicians. These games will be represented by PRISM models, similar to the one presented in this paper, and used in clinical experimentation. Once the models created, we will set up different reference profiles (such as mild, moderate or severe Alzheimer) with the participation of clinicians. Then, several groups of patients will play these games. Their results will be recorded and used to adjust our initial models.

The ultimate goal is to integrate the model checking approach proposed in this paper into a medical monitoring system designed with the help of clinicians.

Acknowledgements. This work is part of the Ph.D. of Thibaud L'Yvonnet. We thank the French Provence-Alpes-Côte d'Azur region for the financial support.

References

1. Ahouandjinou, A.S., Motamed, C., Ezin, E.C.: A temporal belief-based hidden Markov model for human action recognition in medical videos. Pattern Recogn. Image Anal. **25**, 389–401 (2015). https://doi.org/10.1134/S1054661815030025
2. Alur, R., Henzinger, T.: Reactive modules. Formal Methods Syst. Des. **15**, 7–48 (1999). https://doi.org/10.1023/A:1008739929481

3. Atkinson, S.D., Narasimhan, V.L.: Design of an introductory medical gaming environment for diagnosis and management of Parkinson's disease. In: Trendz in Information Sciences Computing (TISC) (2010)

4. Behrmann, G., David, A., Larsen, K.G.: A tutorial on UPPAAL. In: Bernardo, M., Corradini, F. (eds.) SFM-RT 2004. LNCS, vol. 3185, pp. 200–236. Springer, Heidelberg (2004). https://doi.org/10.1007/978-3-540-30080-9_7

5. Buttussi, F., Pellis, T., Cabas-Vidani, A., Pausler, D., Carchietti, E., Chittaro, L.: Evaluation of a 3D serious game for advanced life support retraining. Int. J. Med. Inform. **82**(9), 798–809 (2013)

6. Chamasemani, F.F., Affendey, L.S.: Systematic review and classification on video surveillance systems. Int. J. Inf. Technol. Comput. Sci. (IJITCS) **5**, 87–102 (2013)

7. Chittaro, L., Sioni, R.: Turning the classic snake mobile game into a location–based exergame that encourages walking. In: Bang, M., Ragnemalm, E.L. (eds.) PERSUASIVE 2012. LNCS, vol. 7284, pp. 43–54. Springer, Heidelberg (2012). https://doi.org/10.1007/978-3-642-31037-9_4

8. Clarke, E.M., Grumberg, O., Peled, D.A.: Model Checking. MIT Press, Cambridge (1999)

9. Du, X., El-Khamy, M., Lee, J., Davis, L.: Fused DNN: a deep neural network fusion approach to fast and robust pedestrian detection. In: 2017 IEEE Winter Conference on Applications of Computer Vision (WACV) (2017)

10. Fleming, T.M., et al.: Serious games and gamification for mental health: Current status and promising directions. Front. Psychiatry **7**, 215 (2017)

11. Hansson, H., Jonsson, B.: A logic for reasoning about time and reliability. Formal Aspects Comput. **6**, 512–535 (1994). https://doi.org/10.1007/BF01211866

12. Hassan, M.: A performance model of pedestrian dead reckoning with activity-based location updates. In: 2012 18th IEEE International Conference on Networks (ICON) (2012)

13. Jalal, A., Kamal, S., Kim, D.: A depth video-based human detection and activity recognition using multi-features and embedded hidden Markov models for health care monitoring systems. Int. J. Interact. Multimed. Artif. Intell. **4**(4), 54–62 (2017)

14. Kim, E., Helal, S., Cook, D.: Human activity recognition and pattern discovery. IEEE Pervasive Comput. **9**(1), 48–53 (2009)

15. Kwiatkowska, M., Norman, G., Parker, D.: PRISM 4.0: verification of probabilistic real-time systems. In: Gopalakrishnan, G., Qadeer, S. (eds.) CAV 2011. LNCS, vol. 6806, pp. 585–591. Springer, Heidelberg (2011). https://doi.org/10.1007/978-3-642-22110-1_47

16. Kwiatkowska, M., Norman, G., Parker, D.: Stochastic model checking. In: Bernardo, M., Hillston, J. (eds.) SFM 2007. LNCS, vol. 4486, pp. 220–270. Springer, Heidelberg (2007). https://doi.org/10.1007/978-3-540-72522-0_6

17. Magherini, T., Fantechi, A., Nugent, C.D., Vicario, E.: Using temporal logic and model checking in automated recognition of human activities for ambient-assisted living. IEEE Trans. Hum.-Mach. Syst. **43**(6), 509–521 (2013)

18. Magherini, T., et al.: Temporal logic bounded model-checking for recognition of activities of daily living. In: Proceedings of the 10th IEEE International Conference on Information Technology and Applications in Biomedicine (2010)

19. Nyolt, M., Yordanova, K., Kirste, T.: Checking models for activity recognition. In: ICAART (2015)

20. Piciarelli, C., Canazza, S., Micheloni, C., Foresti, G.L.: A network of audio and video sensors for monitoring large environments. In: Handbook on Soft Computing for Video Surveillance. Chapman & Hall/CRC (2012)

21. Sadigh, D., et al.: Data-driven probabilistic modeling and verification of human driver behavior. In: AAAI Spring Symposium on Formal Verification and Modeling in Human-Machine Systems (FVHMS) (2014)

22. Sun, J., Liu, Y., Dong, J.S., Pang, J.: PAT: towards flexible verification under fairness. In: Bouajjani, A., Maler, O. (eds.) CAV 2009. LNCS, vol. 5643, pp. 709–714. Springer, Heidelberg (2009). https://doi.org/10.1007/978-3-642-02658-4_59

23. Phan Tran, M.K., Bremond, F., Robert, P.: Assistance for older adults in serious game using an interactive system. In: de De Gloria, A., Veltkamp, R. (eds.) GALA 2015. LNCS, vol. 9599, pp. 286–291. Springer, Cham (2016). https://doi.org/10.1007/978-3-319-40216-1_30

24. Ujjwal, U., Dziri, A., Leroy, B., Bremond, F.: Late fusion of multiple convolutional layers for pedestrian detection. In: 15th IEEE International Conference on Advanced Video and Signal-Based Surveillance (AVSS) (2018)

25. Vrigkas, M., Nikou, C., Kakadiaris, I.A.: A review of human activity recognition methods. Front. Robot. AI **2**, 28 (2015)

26. Weerachai, S., Mizukawa, M.: Human behavior recognition via top-view vision for intelligent space. In: International Conference on Control, Automation and Systems (ICCAS) (2010)

27. Zhang, H.B., et al.: A comprehensive survey of vision-based human action recognition methods. Sensors **19**, 1005 (2019)

Tools and Work in Progress

A Framework for Model Checking Against CTLK Using Quantified Boolean Formulas

Emily Yu$^{(\boxtimes)}$, Martina Seidl, and Armin Biere

Institute for Formal Models and Verification, Johannes Kepler University Linz,
Linz, Austria
{zhengqi.yu,martina.seidl,biere}@jku.at

Abstract. We present a novel bounded model checking (BMC) tool chain for multi-agent systems. This framework automatically translates the verification of system models against properties formulated in computation tree logics with epistemic modalities (CTLK) into quantified Boolean formulas (QBFs). Our framework exploits recent QBF technology for solving those verification problems and for certifying the result, making the implementation of a dedicated CTLK solver obsolete. The translation to QBF is based on existing theoretical work and implemented in our novel tool MCMAS$_{\mathsf{qbf}}$ which extends the open-source model checker MCMAS. First experimental results are very promising and indicate the practical feasibility of our approach. Furthermore we provide novel benchmarks to the QBF community.

Keywords: Bounded model checking · QBFs · Multi-agent systems

1 Introduction

Multi-agent systems (MAS) are nowadays applied in various fields to describe complex systems. For example, MAS are used to formalize the interactions of different components that act independently [8]. To verify their correctness, *Computation Tree Logic* with knowledge (CTLK) has been introduced [10]. Besides temporal operators like "**A**lways", "**U**ntil", and "**F**inally", CTLK also includes formulas with knowledge modalities $\mathbf{K}_i\phi$ expressing that "Agent i knows ϕ".

With CTLK it becomes possible to perform model checking for MAS [13]. *Model Checking* [1,5,6] is an important technique for verifying safety-critical systems against properties expressed in temporal logics like LTL or CTL. To deal with the so-called *state explosion problem* of model checking, SAT-based bounded model checking (BMC) [3] was introduced. To obtain more compact encodings of BMC problems than possible with SAT, encodings of BMC to *quantified Boolean formulas* (QBFs) have been presented [7]. Such encodings

This work was supported by the Austrian FWF grant W1255-N23 and the LIT AI Lab funded by the State of Upper Austria.

O. Hasan and F. Mallet (Eds.): FTSCS 2019, CCIS 1165, pp. 127–132, 2020.
https://doi.org/10.1007/978-3-030-46902-3_8

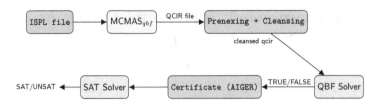

Fig. 1. The complete MCMAS$_{qbf}$ tool chain.

exploit the power of existential and universal quantifiers to avoid duplications of formula parts.

In this paper, we present a fully automatic tool chain for verifying descriptions of multi-agent systems against properties in CTLK. Therefore, we implemented MCMAS$_{qbf}$ for translating such BMC problems to QBFs building upon the bounded semantics of CTLK introduced in [16].

2   The MCMAS$_{qbf}$ Tool Chain

Our tool MCMAS$_{qbf}$ [14] extends MCMAS [12], an open-source model checker for the verification of multi-agent systems supporting various temporal epistemic logics. We reused the parser of MCMAS to obtain the interpreted system data structures based on which we generate the QBF encodings. We implemented the translation of bounded semantics of CTLK into QBFs based on the theoretical work in [16] which includes both existential and universal fragments of the logic. As an approximation to unbounded model checking, the bounded semantics considers a finite state space where each path in the system is restricted to a length of k. However, in the verification process the search space is extended progressively as the formula is evaluated.

The input of MCMAS$_{qbf}$ is an ISPL file which contains a description of the system and a CTLK formula for the property to be checked. ISPL is an agent-based, modular language based on the interpreted systems [9] formalism commonly used for MAS. Our extension is invoked with parameters

$$\texttt{-QBFbmc [k] [QCIR-File] [ISPL-File]},$$

where k is a value specifying the bound followed by an ISPL file and a QCIR output file for the QBF. Our tool MCMAS$_{qbf}$ is embedded in the tool chain as shown in Fig. 1. It produces QBFs in the most general variant of the QCIR format [11], i.e., in non-prenex form which allows to position quantifiers arbitrarily within a formula. Since there is no state-of-the-art QBF solver that supports this general format, an additional prenexing step is necessary to shift the quantifiers to the front. For example, the formula $\forall x \exists y \phi \wedge \forall a \exists b \psi$ has to be rewritten to $\forall a, x \exists b, y (\phi \wedge \psi)$. Therefore, we implemented a simple tool that performs not only quantifier shifting, but also the translation to the cleansed QCIR format that requires the names of the Boolean variables to be numbers and not strings.

Now the QBF can be passed to any QBF solver that is able to process formulas in the cleansed QCIR format. We applied the Quabs [15] that can not only decide the truth value of the formula but also produce certificates. These certificates are And-Inverter-Graphs (AIGs) [4] representing the solution to the BMC problem, and can be checked by a SAT solver for increasing trust in the QBF solver. For this purpose, we use the SAT solver PicoSAT [2].

3   Case Study

As a case study, we consider the popular Train-Gate-Controller (TGC) example [10]. In this scenario, there are multiple trains on different tracks and a controller. The tracks intersect at one tunnel which has red-green lights controlled by the controller, and only one train can operate in the tunnel at a time when the light is green. The following code snippet describes this scenario for one train modeled in ISPL:

```
Agent train1
Vars:
state: {wait, tunnel, away};
end Vars
Actions = {enter, leave, nothing};
Protocol:
state = wait: {enter, nothing};
state = tunnel: {leave, nothing};
state = away: {nothing};
end Protocol
Evolution:
state = wait if state = away and Action = nothing;
state = tunnel if state = wait and Action = enter and Environment.Action=enter1;
state = away if (state = tunnel and Action = leave and Environment.Action=leave1)
or (state=wait and Action=nothing);
end Evolution
end Agent
```

An interpreted system typically contains a set of agents (train1, ...) with possible local states (wait, tunnel, away), actions (enter, leave, nothing), as well as protocols and evolution functions for describing the system behavior. The global states are composed of each agent's local states. Further an initial state is also defined in the ISPL description. To translate the model checking problem into QBFs, we firstly need to encode the interpreted system as follows:

- *state space*: $\lceil \log |L_i| \rceil$ Boolean variables are needed for representing the local states L_i of agent i. The same number of variables is needed for the local successor state. The global current state $\mathbf{v} = (v_e, v_1, ..., v_N)$ and the global successor state $\mathbf{v}' = (v'_e, v'_1, ..., v'_N)$ are vectors of local states where N is the number of agents and e refers to the environment.
- *actions*: For the actions, $\sum_{i \in \{e, 1.., N\}} \lceil \log |Act_i| \rceil$ Boolean variables are needed.
- *transition relation*: For each agent, the protocol function and evolution function are encoded symbolically using v_i and v'_i. The global transition relation is the composition of protocol and evolution functions based on $\mathbf{v}$ and $\mathbf{v}'$.

Table 1. Experimental results obtained for the Train-Gate-Controller case study.

N	k	ϕ_{qbf} (gates)	C	t_{total}(s)	t_{qs}(s)	t_{sat}(s)
3	5	30616	990	0.961	0.056	0.023
3	10	110971	2945	3.445	0.222	0.088
3	15	252226	5950	8.018	0.673	0.201
3	20	464881	10005	14.942	1.178	0.370
5	5	57695	2354	1.785	0.112	0.050
5	10	206735	7299	6.469	0.487	0.156
5	15	464875	14994	15.057	1.261	0.359
5	20	848615	25439	28.560	2.820	0.685
8	5	100482	5480	3.127	0.226	0.084
8	10	357472	17460	11.299	0.982	0.280
8	15	798762	36240	26.195	2.794	0.627
8	20	1449852	61820	51.409	6.882	1.259
10	5	140217	9747	4.607	0.557	0.114
10	10	495812	30452	16.771	2.247	0.389
10	15	1101507	62707	38.680	6.073	0.871
10	20	1988802	106512	76.313	14.219	1.578

We have implemented the encoding presented in [16] and our implementation allows to generate a QBF as a QCIR file which then can be solved and certified by existing QBF solvers. The property holds if the verification result of the QBF solver shows the formula is satisfied, and vice versa.

We verify the following property in our case study: along all paths in the system, it is always the case that if $train_1$ is in the tunnel then it knows that the other trains cannot be operating in the tunnel at the same time. In CTLK, this property can be expressed as follows:

$$\phi = \mathbf{AG}\,(\,\text{in\_tunnel}_1 \;\rightarrow\; \mathbf{K}_{\text{train}_1} \bigvee_{i=2}^{N} \neg\text{in\_tunnel}_i)$$

To evaluate the performance of the tool chain, we ran several experiments on an Intel® Core™ i7-2600 machine with 3.40GHz CPU and 16GB RAM running Ubuntu v18.04.2 (Linux kernel v4.15). We evaluated the bounded model checking problem with different values of k, and in order to test the scalability of the framework, we ran experiments with $5, 8$, and 10 trains (we use N to represent the number of trains).

Table 1 reports the results of our case study. The obtained cleansed QBFs in prenex form contain up to $2M$ gates in the QCIR format, while the certificates in AIGER contain only up to $100K$ gates plus the inputs and outputs related to the QBF variables (C in Table 1). The solving time t_{total} includes the time for the whole tool chain including the QBF solving time t_{qs} and the time for checking the certificates t_{sat}. While the solving times are quite small, much time is needed for the encoding and the cleansing. Here, many optimizations are possible.

4 Discussion

We presented a complete tool chain for solving bounded model checking of multi-agent systems against CTLK specifications using QBF solving technology. First experiments are very promising, allowing us not only to solve the BMC problems but also to obtain quite small certificates from the QBF solvers. Further, this work provides practical benchmarks in the general QCIR format to the QBF community.

As future work, we plan to integrate the model checker with a QBF solver more tightly using an incremental QBF approach to speed up model checking. The translation algorithm can also be optimized further, by for instance picking an arbitrary value of k as a starting point and increase k step-wise in a loop. Furthermore, sub-formulas can be encoded separately then verified, and the verification results can be cached in order to speed up the whole model checking process when applied in a real-world setting.

References

1. Baier, C., Katoen, J.: Principles of Model Checking. MIT Press, Cambridge (2008)
2. Biere, A.: Lingeling, Plingeling, PicoSAT and PrecoSAT at SAT Race 2010. Technical report, FMV Reports Series, Inst. FMV, JKU Linz, Austria (2010)
3. Biere, A., Cimatti, A., Clarke, E., Zhu, Y.: Symbolic model checking without BDDs. In: Cleaveland, W.R. (ed.) TACAS 1999. LNCS, vol. 1579, pp. 193–207. Springer, Heidelberg (1999). https://doi.org/10.1007/3-540-49059-0_14
4. Biere, A., Heljanko, K., Wieringa, S.: AIGER 1.9 and beyond. Technical report, FMV Reports Series, Inst. FMV, JKU Linz, Austria (2011)
5. Clarke, E.M., Grumberg, O., Kroening, D., Peled, D., Veith, H.: Model Checking. MIT press, Cambridge (2018)
6. Clarke, E.M., Henzinger, T.A., Veith, H., Bloem, R. (eds.): Handbook of Model Checking. Springer, Cham (2018). https://doi.org/10.1007/978-3-319-10575-8
7. Dershowitz, N., Hanna, Z., Katz, J.: Bounded model checking with QBF. In: Bacchus, F., Walsh, T. (eds.) SAT 2005. LNCS, vol. 3569, pp. 408–414. Springer, Heidelberg (2005). https://doi.org/10.1007/11499107_32
8. Dorri, A., Kanhere, S.S., Jurdak, R.: Multi-agent systems: a survey. IEEE Access 6, 28573–28593 (2018)
9. Fagin, R., Halpern, J.Y., Moses, Y., Vardi, M.Y.: Reasoning About Knowledge. MIT Press, Cambridge (2003)
10. van der Hoek, W., Wooldridge, M.J.: Tractable multiagent planning for epistemic goals. In: AAMAS, pp. 1167–1174. ACM (2002)
11. Jordan, C., Klieber, W., Seidl, M.: Non-CNF QBF solving with QCIR. In: AAAI Workshop: Beyond NP, vol. WS-16-05. AAAI Press (2016)

12. Lomuscio, A., Qu, H., Raimondi, F.: MCMAS: a model checker for the verification of multi-agent systems. In: Bouajjani, A., Maler, O. (eds.) CAV 2009. LNCS, vol. 5643, pp. 682–688. Springer, Heidelberg (2009). https://doi.org/10.1007/978-3-642-02658-4_55

13. Lomuscio, A., Raimondi, F.: The complexity of model checking concurrent programs against CTLK specifications. In: Baldoni, M., Endriss, U. (eds.) DALT 2006. LNCS (LNAI), vol. 4327, pp. 29–42. Springer, Heidelberg (2006). https://doi.org/10.1007/11961536_3

14. MCMAS-QBF (2019). http://fmv.jku.at/ftscs19

15. Tentrup, L.: Non-prenex QBF solving using abstraction. In: Creignou, N., Le Berre, D. (eds.) SAT 2016. LNCS, vol. 9710, pp. 393–401. Springer, Cham (2016). https://doi.org/10.1007/978-3-319-40970-2_24

16. Zhou, C., Chen, Z., Tao, Z.: QBF-based symbolic model checking for knowledge and time. In: Cai, J.-Y., Cooper, S.B., Zhu, H. (eds.) TAMC 2007. LNCS, vol. 4484, pp. 386–397. Springer, Heidelberg (2007). https://doi.org/10.1007/978-3-540-72504-6_35

Formal Semantics Extraction from MIPS Instruction Manual

Quang Thinh Trac$^{(\boxtimes)}$ and Mizuhito Ogawa$^{(\boxtimes)}$

Japan Advanced Institute of Science and Technology, Nomi, Ishikawa, Japan
{tracthinh,mizuhito}@jaist.ac.jp

Abstract. This study proposes a semi-automatic extraction of the formal semantics of MIPS architecture from the pseudocode description in MIPS instruction manual. Among 127 collected instructions, we focus on the 63 instructions of the CPU category. After manually preparing 21 primitive functions in the pseudocode description, their semantics are successfully generated as Java methods, which are unified to a dynamic symbolic execution tool SyMIPS. We perform an empirical study on 3219 MIPS32 IoT malware collected from ViruSign and observe that SyMIPS successfully traces 2412 samples, in which SyMIPS finds the dead conditional branch, e.g., in DDOS-Y. The rest is interrupted by either timeout, stack overflow, or exceptions, which current SyMIPS does not cover.

Keywords: Dynamic symbolic execution · MIPS32 · IoT malware

1 Introduction

Symbolic execution has been developed mostly for high-level programming languages, e.g., JPF-SE [1] for Java and Klee [4] for C. Recently, symbolic execution tools are extended to binary code. An early example is McVeto [11], followed by KLEE-MC [2], Mayhem [5], MiAsm [6], CoDisasm [3], BE-PUM [9], Angr [10], Corana [13]. Most of them are developed for x86 except Corana for ARM.

When we consider IoT devices, various architectures exist. Smaller CPUs, MPU (Micro Processor Unit), are either 32 bits or 64 bits, e.g., ARM Cortex-A, MIPS32, MIPS64, MC68000, Sparc (by Fujitsu), PowerPC, and x86. Controllers, MCU (Micro Controller Unit), are up to 32 bits, e.g., ARM Cortex-M7, Z80, PIC, AVR, MSP430 (TI), and RL78 (Runesas). When we develop binary symbolic execution tools, the large variation forces huge human effort. Good news is:

1. Each instruction set often has a concrete manual in rigid English.
2. MPUs and MCUs have shallow caches and mostly do not allow out-of-order execution. Avoiding multi-threads, weak memory models, and floating-point arithmetic, the operational semantics framework simply becomes the transitions on the environment consisting of *memory*, *stack*, *registers*, and *flags*.
3. Various debuggers and emulators are often available, which implement the semantics of instruction sets.

© Springer Nature Switzerland AG 2020
O. Hasan and F. Mallet (Eds.): FTSCS 2019, CCIS 1165, pp. 133–140, 2020.
https://doi.org/10.1007/978-3-030-46902-3_9

They suggest (semi-)automatic extraction of the formal semantics from English manuals. Furthermore, by comparing with the execution between existing debuggers/emulators and the generated symbolic execution tool, the conformance testing can resolve the ambiguity in natural language processing.

For extracting the semantics, the following three sections are essential.

- Format section shows the name of the instruction and its operands.
- Operation section shows how the environment is updated. Some instruction sets also have the pseudo-code descriptions, e.g., x86 and MIPS.
- Flag Update section shows the change of the boolean condition. Some instruction sets have no flags, e.g., MIPS, and the condition is set on registers.

Following to BE-PUM for x86 [8] and Corana for ARM [13]), this study investigates a semi-automatic extraction of the formal semantics of MIPS instructions. Among MIPS variations, we focus on MIPS32 (release 5) from MIPS32 instruction set manual[1], which has the emulator MARS. Among 127 collected MIPS32 instruction specifications, we focus on 63 of the CPU category. After preparing a Java template describing the operational semantics framework, we manually prepare 21 primitive functions in the pseudocode description, which successfully instantiate the Java template for all 63 instructions. The generated Java code is inserted into a dynamic symbolic execution tool SyMIPS[2]. We perform an empirical study on 3219 MIPS32 IoT malware in ViruSign[3] and observe that SyMIPS successfully traces 2412 samples. The rest is interrupted by either timeout, stack overflow, or exceptions, which current SyMIPS does not cover. Note that SyMIPS finds the dead conditional branch, e.g., in DDOS-Y.

1.1   Related Work

The first trial of a formal semantics extraction appears for x86 [8] for extending BE-PUM [9], which introduced the sentence-level similarity analysis to detect flag updates. The experiment shows that among 530 collected specifications from Intel Developer's Manual[4], Java method descriptions of 299×86 instructions are successfully generated by manually preparing 30 primitive functions, which not only enlarged the BE-PUM support to the total 400 instructions but also found 5 human bugs in manually implemented 200 instructions.

The formal semantics extraction for ARM [13] is more challenging, since the ARM manual is described only in English. By manually preparing 228 semantics interpretation rules, the experiment shows that among 1039 collected ARM Cortex-M specifications from ARM manual[5], 662 instructions are successfully processed. Note that both apply the conformance testing by using the existing emulators, i.e., Ollydbg[6] for x86 and μVision[7] for ARM.

---

[1] https://www.mips.com/products/architectures/mips32-2.
[2] https://github.com/tracquangthinh/SyMIPS.
[3] https://www.virusign.com.
[4] https://www.felixcloutier.com/x86.
[5] https://developer.arm.com.
[6] http://www.ollydbg.de.
[7] http://keil.com/mdk5/uvision.

2   Formal Semantics of MIPS

2.1   MIPS Architecture

MIPS is a RISC instruction set, which were introduced in 1985. MIPS assumes a load/store architecture (or known as register-register architecture, in which the memory access is limited to the load and store instructions. A conventional MIPS processor contains the following components:

1. **Registers**: is a small set of high-speed storage cells inside the CPU. MIPS provides 32 general-purpose registers.
2. **Memory**: is the 32-bits addressing space.
3. **Stack**: is taken as a special area of the memory.

In contrast to x86 and ARM, MIPS have no flags. Instead, it uses general registers for storing the boolean conditions. Furthermore, the MIPS instructions except for the load/store, `lb`, `sb`, `lw`, `sw`, cannot directly access memory.

2.2   MIPS Instruction Manual

The specification of the MIPS instructions is collected and extracted from the MIPS32 (release 5) instruction set manual. They are in the PDF format and consist of four prime sections including `format`, `purpose`, `description` and `operation`. Table below shows an example of the specification of instruction `ADDI`. Among four sections, `format` and `operation` are used to obtain Java methods.

Format	ADDI rt, rs, immediate
Purpose	To add a constant to a 32-bit integer. If overflow occurs, then trap.

Description	The 16-bit signed immediate is added to the 32-bit value in GPR rs to produce a 32-bit result.
	  – If the addition results in 32-bit 2's complement arithmetic overflow, the destination register is not modified and an Integer Overflow exception occurs.
	  – If the addition does not overflow, the 32-bit result is placed into GPR rt.

Operation	`temp ← (rs[31]||rs[31..0]) + sign_extend(immediate)`
	`if temp[32] ≠ temp[31] then`
	` SignalException(IntegerOverflow)`
	`else`
	` rt ← sign_extend(temp[31..0])`
	`endif`

2.3   Java Methods as Formal Semantics

We describe the formal semantics of MIPS instructions by Java methods with a Java class BitVec, originally prepared for Corana [13]. The value of the BitVec class is a pair $\langle bs, s \rangle$, where bs is a 32-bit vector variable in the BitSet class and s is a string variable that stores a symbolic value in the BitVector theory. We manually prepare 21 primitive functions appearing in the pseudocode. An example below is a generated Java method of the instruction ADDI

```
public void ADDI(Character rt, Character rs,
                    int immediate){
    BitVec temp = add(concat(val(rs).get(31),
                    val(rs).get(0, 31)), signExtend(immediate));
    if(notEqual(temp.get(32), temp.get(31))){
        signalException(IntegerOverflow);
    } else { write(rt,signExtend(temp.get(0, 31))); }
}
```

3   Specification Extraction

3.1   Operation Extraction

The operation section describes the pseudo-code. It is the most important field for extracting MIPS formal semantics and generating Java executable code. However, MIPS Instruction Set manual obeys general common knowledge on the syntax and the semantics of the pseudo-code. Following to x86 formal semantics extraction [8], we manually prepare a context-free grammar including 17 rules for parsing the pseudo-code. We used ANTLR (ANother Tool for Language Recognition)[8] to generate a parser, which results the abstract syntax tree.

Representation of BitVector Theory. String variables are used to store values in BitVector theory of the SMT format and the primitive functions compute 32-bit values. Below is an example of a primitive function **and**.

```
BitVec and(BitVec m, BitVec n) {
    String symbolic = "(bvand "+ m.symbolic +
                    " " + n.symbolic + ")";
    BitSet concrete = m.and(n);
    return new BitVec(concrete, symbolic); }
```

---

[8] https://www.antlr.org.

3.2   Conformance Testing

JDart [7] is a dynamic symbolic tool built on the top of Java PathFinder [12]. After converting the pseudo-code to Java methods, we use JDart to generate the test cases of Java methods to cover all feasible execution paths of MIPS instructions. Then we apply the conformance testing by comparing the executed results of Java methods and MARS[9] - a trusted emulator of MIPS32.

1. Apply JDart for the symbolic execution on a generated Java method, and generate test cases to cover its all feasible branches.
2. Execute the generated Java method and the instruction on the trusted emulator MARS with all generated test cases, and compare their results.

4   Dynamic Execution Tool: SyMIPS

A preliminary version of a dynamic symbolic execution tool SyMIPS[10] (**Sy**mbolic Execution for **MIPS**) adopts Capstone (as a single-step disassembler) and Z3[11] (as a backend SMT solver).

4.1   Environment Updates

SyMIPS updates the environment and the path condition when executing an instruction, based on the BitVec class and 21 primitive methods (Sect. 2.3). For instance, `ADDI r2, r3, 3` set r2 to r3 + 3 and updates symbolic values. For the BitSet value c_i and the symbolic values s_i with $i \in \{2, 3\}$, the pre-environment `preEnv` $r_2 : \langle c_2, s_2 \rangle$; $r_3 : \langle c_3, s_3 \rangle$ is updated to the post-environment `postEnv`

$$
\begin{aligned}
r_2 : \quad & \langle c_3 + 3, ((\_\, sign\_extend\ 1)((\_\, extract\ 30\ 0)(bvadd\ (concat \\
& ((\_\, extract\ 31\ 31)\ r_3)((\_\, extract\ 30\ 0)\ r_3))\ \#x00000003)))) \rangle \\
r_3 : \quad & \langle c_3 \quad , s_3 \rangle
\end{aligned}
$$

4.2   Path Conditions Generation

The path condition is updated when a conditional jump occurs. Returning to the example above, we assume that the next instruction is `beq r2 r4 offset` while `offset` is the destination of the jump instruction. This instruction `beq` compares two registers r2 and r4, then if r2 equals to r4, it branches to the offset. The path conditions of the true and false branches are updated as:

---

[9] http://courses.missouristate.edu/KenVollmar/mars.
[10] https://github.com/tracquangthinh/SyMIPS.
[11] https://github.com/Z3Prover/z3.

$$\text{pc}_{\text{true}} = \quad pc \wedge (= ((\_\, sign\_extend\ 1)((\_\, extract\ 30\ 0)$$
$$(bvadd(concat\ ((\_\, extract\ 31\ 31)\ r_3)$$
$$((\_\, extract\ 30\ 0)\ r_3))\ \#x00000003)))\ r_4)$$

$$\text{pc}_{\text{false}} = \quad pc \wedge (not\ (= ((\_\, sign\_extend\ 1)((\_\, extract\ 30\ 0)$$
$$(bvadd\ (concat\ ((\_\, extract\ 31\ 31)\ r_3)$$
$$((\_\, extract\ 30\ 0)\ r_3))\ \#x00000003)))\ r_4))$$

4.3 SyMIPS Versus BE-PUM, Corana

BE-PUM was originally implemented manually and later the formal semantics extraction of 299×86 instructions extends BE-PUM [8]. Compared to BE-PUM, SyMIPS and Corana are generated from scratch and share the use of the `BitVec` class. However, there are several differences:

1. ARM uses the flags and the conditional suffix to implement conditional executions. In contrast, MIPS only uses general registers.
2. ARM instructions treat 32-bit general registers as the word-size values and do not require to access single bits during the execution. Meanwhile, MIPS handles registers in the level of bits by producing `get` as a primitive function. For instance, the `ADDI` instruction uses a conditional statement to decide whether an overflow occurs. By using the `get` function, `ADDI` accesses the 31st and 32th single bits of the temporary variable `temp`.

5 Experiments and Results

5.1 SyMIPS Performance

We perform experiments on MIPS32 IoT malware (taken from ViruSign) to see the performance of SyMIPS. Note that current SyMIPS implementation is preliminary. We try 3219 samples on Ubuntu 18.04 with Intel Core i5-6200U CPU, 2.30 GHz and 8 GB. The results are summarized below.

Types of Executions		Number of samples
Finished		2412
Interrupted	Out of Memory	415
	Jump to Kernel Space/ System Calls	79
	Fail to read binary format	313
Total		3219
Average Size		178.8 KB

Range(seconds)	Number of Samples	Size(KBs)			Execution Time		
		Min	Max	Average	Min	Max	Average
0 - 10	1658	0.5	638	165			
10 - 20	941	30	763	111			
20 - 30	155	47	198	138			
30 - 40	36	59	240	153	1.21	991.22	17.46
40 - 50	154	121	301	200			
50 - 60	74	142	1156	312			
>60	201	124	531	292			

5.2 Handling Dynamic Jumps by SyMIPS

Although IoT malware rarely uses obfuscation techniques, identifying the destination of indirect jumps is essential to understand the control structure.

```
0x401898    lw t9, -0x7fe0(gp)
0x40189c    nop                        0x4004e8    slti v0, v0, 2
0x4018a0    addiu t9, t9, 0x19bc       0x4004ec    beqz v0, 0x40049c
0x4018a4    jalr t9                    0x4004f0    nop
0x4019c8    addiu sp, sp, -0x20        0x4004f4    lw v1, 0x44(fp)
0x4019cc    sw ra, 0x18(sp)            0x4004f8    addiu v0, zero, 1
   (a) Trace of the indirect jump        (b) The true branch is UNSAT
```

Indirect Jump. Example (a) shows an indirect jump jalr at 0x4018a4 in ELF:Mirai-ACL. SyMIPS finds the destination 0x4019c8 by concolic testing.

Conditional Jump. Example. (b) shows a conditional jump beqz at 0x4004ec in ELF:DDoS-Y. SyMIPS detects that the true branch is unsatisfiable. It always goes to 0x4004f0 and the code fragment starting at 0x40049c is dead code.

6 Conclusion

We proposed a semi-automatic formal semantics extraction of MIPS32 instructions from their manual. Consequently, a preliminary version of a dynamic symbolic execution tool SyMIPS for MIPS32 was presented. The experiments on 3219 IoT malware taken from ViruSign successfully analyzed 2412 samples, including the detection of dead conditional branches, e.g., in DDOS-Y.

Acknowledgement. This study is partially supported by JSPS KAKENHI Grant-in-Aid for Scientific Research (B)19H04083. The original content was accepted as the master thesis [14].

References

1. Anand, S., Păsăreanu, C.S., Visser, W.: JPF–SE: a symbolic execution extension to Java pathfinder. In: Grumberg, O., Huth, M. (eds.) TACAS 2007. LNCS, vol. 4424, pp. 134–138. Springer, Heidelberg (2007). https://doi.org/10.1007/978-3-540-71209-1_12

2. Anthony, R.: Methods for binary symbolic execution. Ph.D Dissertation, Stanford University, December 2014
3. Bonfante, G., Fernandez, J., Marion, J.Y., Rouxel, B., Sabatier, F., Thierry, A.: CoDisasm: medium scale concatic disassembly of self-modifying binaries with overlapping instructions. In: ACM SIGSAC, pp. 745–756 (2015)
4. Cadar, C., Dunbar, D., Engler, D.: KLEE: unassisted and automatic generation of high-coverage tests for complex systems programs. In: OSDI (2009)
5. Cha, S.K., Avgerinos, T., Rebert, A., Brumley, D.: Unleashing Mayhem on binary code. In: IEEE S&P, pp. 380–394 (2012)
6. Desclaux, F.: Miasm: framework de reverse engineering (2012)
7. Luckow, K., et al.: JDart: a dynamic symbolic analysis framework. In: TACAS, pp. 442–459 (2016)
8. Nguyen, H.L.Y.: Automatic extraction of x86 formal semantics from its natural language description. Master's Thesis, School of Information Science, JAIST, March 2018
9. Nguyen, M.H., Ogawa, M., Quan, T.T.: Obfuscation code localization based on CFG generation of malware. In: FPS, pp. 229–247 (2015)
10. Shoshitaishvili, Y., et al.: (State of) the art of war: offensive techniques in binary analysis. In: IEEE S&P, pp. 138–157 (2016)
11. Thakur, A., et al.: Directed proof generation for machine code. In: Touili, T., Cook, B., Jackson, P. (eds.) CAV 2010. LNCS, vol. 6174, pp. 288–305. Springer, Heidelberg (2010). https://doi.org/10.1007/978-3-642-14295-6_27
12. Visser, W., Havelund, K., Brat, G., Park, S.: Model checking programs. In: IEEE ASE, pp. 3–11 (2000)
13. Vu, A.V., Ogawa, M.: Formal semantics extraction from natural language specifications for ARM. In: ter Beek, M.H., McIver, A., Oliveira, J.N. (eds.) FM 2019. LNCS, vol. 11800, pp. 465–483. Springer, Cham (2019). https://doi.org/10.1007/978-3-030-30942-8_28
14. Trac, Q.T.: Generating a dynamic symbolic execution tool from MIPS specifiations. Master's Thesis, School of Information Science, JAIST, September 2019

Author Index

Printed in the United States
By Bookmasters